# The Numerical Methods
# Programming Projects Book

# The Numerical Methods Programming Projects Book

## THOMAS A. GRANDINE

*University of Wisconsin, Madison*

Oxford   New York   Tokyo
OXFORD UNIVERSITY PRESS
1990

Oxford University Press, Walton Street, Oxford OX2 6DP

Oxford New York Toronto
Delhi Bombay Calcutta Madras Karachi
Petaling Jaya Singapore Hong Kong Tokyo
Nairobi Dar es Salaam Cape Town
Melbourne Auckland
and associated companies in
Berlin Ibadan

Oxford is a trade mark of Oxford University Press

Published in the United States
by Oxford University Press, New York

British Library Cataloguing in Publication Data
Grandine, Thomas A.
The numerical methods programming projects book.
1. Numerical analysis. Applications of computer systems
I. Title
519.4
ISBN 0–19–853385–3
ISBN 0–19–853387–X (Pbk)

Library of Congress Cataloging in Publication Data
Data available

Printed in Great Britain
by Courier International, Tiptree, Essex

# Preface

This book is a collection of programming projects I have assigned to the students in my Introduction to Numerical Methods class at the University of Wisconsin—Madison over the last three semesters. It has been my hope that the students have had as much fun working on these projects as I have had in making them up. These projects represent my attempt to design programming problems which combine real-world events and fictitious enterprises in a humorous fashion. The result is this collection of twenty-two different projects which have a common theme, namely to aid and assist ACME in matters technical, legal, and bureaucratic.

I have tried, whenever possible, to use physically correct mathematical models in all of the projects, especially when differential equations are involved. Sadly, I have failed to do this in Project 13 and again in Project 14, where completely phony equations have been introduced solely for the purpose of complicating the computations. In addition, the measurements obtained in Project 16 are completely artificial. Most of the other situations, while certainly made up, at least make physical sense, even if no other sense is made.

In preparing this book, I have received much advice and assistance. Project 8 and Project 12 were actually written by John Strikwerda, who taught another section of the same course during the second of the three semesters. In addition, one of his technical summary reports is the basis for Project 20, which deals with the manufacture of optic fibers. He has also made several other suggestions and improvements to many of the projects. Scott Markel and Bruce Wade also gave me much editorial assistance as well as a great deal of encouragement. The computer time that I needed in order to test my own problems and make sure that they were well-posed was provided by the Mathematics Research Center under US Army Contract No. DAAG29–80–C–0041. Yvonne Nagel helped with the typesetting by helping me to understand some of the intricacies of TeX.

I owe a special debt of gratitude to Karl Knapp of the Numerical Algorithms Group, Inc. He generously provided a copy of the NAG FORTRAN Library for the students in the class to use. He also proofread the entire manuscript and helped me to clarify a few of my instructions. Additionally, he wrote the programs which use the NAG Graphical Library and provided the documentation for the NAG FORTRAN Workstation Library, both of which form the basis for two of the appendices. This project would never have been undertaken without his continual encouragement.

No list of acknowledgements would be complete without mentioning the students, who, for the last three semesters, have patiently tolerated long nights in the terminal room, high load averages, several system crashes, and my strange sense of humor. They survived it all with very little complaining.

*Madison, Wisconsin*                                                                    T. G.
May 1986

# Contents

# Introduction

## Why use this book?

The projects in this book are intended to accomplish several things. The first is to present numerical computations in a context in which they might actually occur. Thus, the students, under the guise of completing various tasks for a fictitious company, gain insight into the role that numerical methods play in science and industry. The projects are all constructed so that the solutions have physical meaning for the particular problem which must be solved. In addition, the problems occasionally require two or more numerical methods in order to obtain the solution. This means that the projects are occasionally unpredictable: a student never knows exactly when a numerical method discussed earlier in the course is going to be required to solve a current problem. This global view of the subject makes it possible for the student to realize that real-world problems are never as straightforward as many textbooks would have you believe. Thus, an appreciation for the relevancy of the material is enhanced.

The second goal of these projects is to get students used to the idea of using good numerical software when writing numerical programs. Even though coursework itself is often very much a description of how to build various numerical black boxes, the projects here concentrate on some of the applications of those black boxes. Thus, students who attempt to complete many of these projects will find it nearly impossible to do so in a reasonable amount of time unless a good numerical software library is relied upon. Students tend to be more impressed with numerical solutions to sophisticated problems than with simple-minded solutions to meaningless test problems. This also helps to foster the notion that numerical methods are an important tool in the students' problem-solving arsenal.

The third goal of these projects is to add a light touch to what many students consider a colorless subject, full of dull convergence proofs and repetitive error estimates. An attempt has been made to liven all of this up with silly acronyms, absurd situations, foolish jargon, and science fictional devices. This seeming irreverence serves as motivation, and it accomplishes what might be difficult otherwise. Because the entire project is described in entertaining terms, students are much less inclined to be intimidated by an otherwise difficult assignment. Playing along with the game seems to keep everyone from taking things too seriously, which is as sure a hindrance to learning as not taking things seriously enough.

These projects are of mixed difficulty. They range from the trivial and straightforward (Project 1) to the challenging and complex (Project 22). It is by no means expected that all of these should be completed in one-term. For this reason, no project depends upon the results or the jargon of any previous project, although occasionally some of the characters reappear. Most of the topics covered in a typical one-term numerical methods course are covered in the problems. The following table is a quick summary of the contents and difficulty of each of the projects:

| Project | Content | Difficulty |
| --- | --- | --- |
| 1 | Floating point arithmetic | Easy |
| 2 | Floating point arithmetic | Easy |
| 3 | Floating point arithmetic | Easy to moderate |
| 4 | Polynomial interpolation | Easy to moderate |
| 5 | Polynomial interpolation | Moderate |
| 6 | Rootfinding | Easy to moderate |
| 7 | Rootfinding | Moderate |
| 8 | Linear equations | Moderate |
| 9 | Linear equations | Easy to moderate |
| 10 | Linear equations | Moderate |
| 11 | Linear least-squares | Easy |
| 12 | Linear equations | Hard |
| 13 | Rootfinding | Moderate to hard |
| 14 | Differential equations, rootfinding | Moderate to hard |
| 15 | Quadrature, spline interpolation | Moderate |
| 16 | Quadrature, linear equations | Easy to moderate |
| 17 | Differential equations | Easy |
| 18 | Differential equations | Easy to moderate |
| 19 | Differential equations | Moderate |
| 20 | Differential equations | Moderate to hard |
| 21 | Differential equations | Hard |
| 22 | Spline approximation, optimization | Very hard |

# Why use a software library?

For most numerical programming tasks, the use of a solid, robust software library improves computational results and minimizes programmer effort. These days, a programmer who wants results in a reasonable amount of time won't even consider writing a large code in assembly language; his results would take too long to obtain and would be more prone to error. High-level programming languages are therefore used to save time and minimize the number of bugs that occur in a program.

Sadly, these packages often are not used. Gaussian elimination routines have been programmed countless times, as have various simple-minded quadrature formulas, even when excellent routines are already available on the system being used. There are many reasons for this, which need not be discussed here. Suffice it to say that it happens. The net effect, unfortunately, is that people to write their own numerical subroutines based on examples in books rather than trust routines written by strangers, even when the strangers happen to be experts.

This may be an understandable attitude. It does not, however, lead to an effective technique for carrying out the numerical solution to problems. A carpenter would not dream of going to the forge to construct his own hammer, unless he happened to have some project in mind for which the available hammers simply weren't adequate. He would be content to obtain a hammer from the local hardware store, and he would then trust it to accomplish what he had in mind. The important lesson in all of this is that even though it is important for a carpenter to understand how a hammer works, it is seldom necessary for him to manufacture his own.

Numerical programmers should adopt this attitude more often. While it is often essential to understand how various numerical methods work, it is not essential nor a good idea to construct subroutines based on these methods when excellent subroutines which accomplish the same thing are so readily available. Numerical software should be viewed as an effective tool for performing many different computations whose use often requires some knowledge of numerical methods.

In this book, the Numerical Algorithms Group (NAG) software library has been used. This library is by no means the only available numerical software library, but it is typical of many of them in most respects. The NAG FORTRAN Library is a collection of some 688 user-callable FORTRAN routines. The routines used in this book also belong to the NAG FORTRAN Workstation Library, a subset of 172 of the most commonly used routines in the NAG FORTRAN Library. This means that the projects in this book can be completed even on various microcomputers. The documentation for NAG is also of very high quality, making it especially suitable as a learning tool. The documentation for the NAG routines which are used in this book can be found in Appendix C.

For the sake of continuity, the use of one of the NAG libraries is strongly recommended for the projects in this book. However, there is no reason why they can't be done just as effectively using some other library.

The following NAG routines (which are part of the NAG FORTRAN Workstation Library) are needed for the projects:

| | |
|---|---|
| C05ADF | Zeroes of functions of one variable |
| D01AJF | Numerical integration |
| D02BBF | Numerical solution of initial-value problems |
| D02HBF | Numerical solution of boundary-value problems |
| E02BAF | Cubic spline interpolation |
| E02BCF | Cubic spline evaluation |
| E02BDF | Cubic spline integration |
| E04VDF | Non-linear constrained optimization |
| F01BTF | LU factorization of a matrix |
| F02WAF | Singular value decomposition of a matrix |
| F04AYF | Numerical solution of linear equations |
| F04JGF | QR factorization of a matrix |

The routines E02BAF and F02WAF can be replaced by E01BAF and F02WCF, respectively, if these are available. (They are part of the NAG FORTRAN Library, but not the NAG FORTRAN Workstation Library). The two replacements are more convenient to use in the situations in which they are required.

## Why use FORTRAN?

Despite what terrible things you may have heard about FORTRAN, and despite what unpleasant personal experiences you may have had with it, the nature of numerical programming generally makes its use a good idea. There are several reasons for this, one of the most compelling being that most of the major numerical software libraries, including the NAG FORTRAN Library, are written in FORTRAN. This certainly facilitates the passing of parameters.

However, this is not the only compelling reason to program in FORTRAN. FORTRAN is built with numerical computation in mind. Most good compilers are optimizing compilers, which means that they produce very fast code. For applications which are computation intensive, which numerical programs are, the final code will often run several times faster if it is written in FORTRAN than it will if it is written in C, PASCAL, MODULA, PL/1, or any other structured language. In addition, FORTRAN compilers are often constructed to take advantage of special computational hardware and various floating point processors which are available on some machines. The performance of the final code is often of crucial importance in numerical applications.

In addition, FORTRAN supports complex arithmetic. While many other languages have the potential for accommodating this, few have it built right into the language in as natural a way as it is in FORTRAN. Much care has been taken in the construction of intrinsic functions as well, so the computations often tend to be more reliable if there are calls to transcendental functions present in the program. The designers of other language compilers have many users to satisfy, and the needs of the numerical analysts are often overlooked in the construction of compilers. It is the job of the FORTRAN compiler writer, however, to guarantee that his compiler performs numerical computations as well as possible.

All of this means that it is now the responsibility of the FORTRAN programmer to discipline himself. Even though FORTRAN allows things like undeclared variables, unrestrained use of GO TO statements, poor programming style, etc., these are bad programming practices and should be avoided. FORTRAN is a pleasant language in which to work, but it does require somewhat more self-restraint than the various structured programming languages. The programmer must be willing to impose this self-restraint.

# The setup

As a recent graduate of the Binary Institute of Technology, one of the leading institutions of science and engineering in the world, you have just entered the job market. After locating the college placement office on the campus BIT map, you have wandered in to begin your search for an exciting and challenging career. The people there have scheduled several interviews for you, and you have begun your job search by talking to representatives of several big companies.

After careful consideration of the dozen or more job offers which are currently in front of you, you have decided to accept the job with the Applied Computational Mathematics and Engineering Company. ACME is a huge international corporation with many very diverse interests. Some of these are computers, energy, construction, pharmaceuticals, chemicals, mineral exploration, and oceanography.

You are employed by the Subdivision On Large, Vincible Exercises. It is the job of SOLVE to act primarily as a consulting group for the rest of ACME. Whenever someone at ACME has a problem which proves too difficult to tackle, SOLVE is called upon. It will be your responsibility as an employee of SOLVE to be one of the general trouble-shooters and consultants who help out throughout all of ACME.

Your boss, Biro Kratt, knows nothing about computers or mathematics, so he will be relying heavily on you to handle the problems which might come up in this area. Fortunately, you took a numerical methods course at BIT, so you feel confident of your ability not only to get the job done, but to get it done well.

Some of the projects which you will be assigned will be easy, while others will be difficult. Each project will describe some situation which could conceivably occur in the real world. Thus, the formulation of the problem itself is occasionally the hardest part of the whole project. Very often, you will be given extraneous information, and you will have to decide which information is important, and which should be disregarded.

For each project, you will be asked to write a program in FORTRAN. This program should be documented well, with enough comments included so that a first-time reader of your program can get a fairly good idea of what your program is doing and how it is doing it. In addition, you will be asked to prepare a project summary for each project. This summary should describe everything that you did on the project: how you decided to solve the problem, what your program does and is capable of doing, what the numbers produced by your program mean, and any other information which is relevant to the particular project. The project summary is one of the most important parts of any project; be sure to treat it that way.

Your career with ACME promises to be entertaining, challenging, and occasionally demanding. If you work hard, it will be rewarding, too.

# Project 1

Someone at ACME has made a mistake. While you are still relatively new to the company, it will be your job to fix this error. In the code for the Brainy Useful Gadget, a device which ACME is currently building for the military, there appears the following useless routine, purchased from ACME for the sum of $100,000:

```
        PROGRAM RAID

        REAL A, B
        INTEGER K

        A = 2416.1953
        B = 2416.1952

        K = 0
        IF (A .NE. B) K = 1

        WRITE (6,601) K, A, B
601     FORMAT (1X,'K = ',I3,',', 2416.1953 = ',F12.6,/
      *                     9X,' 2416.1952 = ',F12.6)

        END
```

The BUG is a fully functioning device, at least in terms of what it was designed to do. Nevertheless, your predecessor was unable to explain the behavior of this routine (hence the reason for his dismissal). Your boss would really like to know just why this routine for the BUG works the way it does on 32 bit machines. Check it out on your computer and explain the results.

Once this nuisance has been cleared up, you are to begin helping the project team working on ACME's newest product, the Humble Automatic Lackey 9000, a new industrial robot which is currently in the design phase. ACME's HAL–9000 is almost complete, but some of its functions have not yet been implemented. Your job will be to write the firmware for the $\sin \pi x$ function, which is necessary for positioning HAL's arm. Since HAL has a tendency to take matters into his own hands, it is important that this function be implemented properly. The best way to do this, of course, is to call the FORTRAN SIN function. However, your boss, who, as you will recall, knows very little mathematics, insists that you use the Taylor series. Remember that the Taylor series for this function is given by

$$\sin \pi x = \pi x - \frac{\pi^3 x^3}{3!} + \frac{\pi^5 x^5}{5!} - \frac{\pi^7 x^7}{7!} + \dots$$

Write a FORTRAN program to do the computations. Your program should read in a value for $x$ and then add successive terms of the Taylor series until the sum does not change when the next term is added. It should keep track of how many terms have been added. For output, you should print out the value of $x$, the number of terms needed in the Taylor series, the value for $\sin \pi x$ obtained by your program, and the value obtained by using FORTRAN's SIN function. You are doing this last step because you are skeptical about your boss's approach to this problem. Run this program for the following values of $x$: 0.1, 2.1, 4.1, 6.1, 8.1, 10.1, 15.1, and 20.1.

You should notice that your routine works reasonably well for some values of $x$, but very poorly for others. Explain to your boss why his approach to this problem works the way it does. You should do this by handing in a listing of your program, the output it produced, and a written explanation of the results. In doing all of this, remember what happened to your predecessor at ACME. You may find the following hints helpful:

**Hint 1:** When computing $n!$, you should be aware that even moderate values for $n$ are likely to cause an overflow. You might wish to consider the following equation:

$$\frac{x^n}{n!} = \left( \frac{x^{n-1}}{(n-1)!} \right) \left( \frac{x}{n} \right).$$

**Hint 2:** Use a decent value for $\pi$. Since it is often difficult to know just what machine precision is for any given machine, formulas such as the following should always be used to obtain a value for $\pi$:

$$\pi = \cos^{-1}(-1)$$
$$= 4 \tan^{-1}(1)$$

The FORTRAN functions ACOS and ATAN can be used for this purpose. In addition, the NAG routine X01AAF can also be used. Since there is some work involved here, $\pi$ should be computed only once and stored in a variable.

**Hint 3:** Since it is often impossible to predict in advance the magnitude of the numbers computed, you should use a suitable format statement in your program. Try using 'e' format with an appropriate number of digits.

# Project 2

---

SOLVE has just been asked to help out the Computer Operations Network For Useful Synthesis of Engineering Devices, a division of ACME which builds small electronic devices. CONFUSED has a new project currently in the mill: they are building the new ACME Widget For Useful Logarithms, a simple scientific calculator. You have been asked to help out the project team designing the AWFUL. Your particular task is to design the firmware for the $e^x$ key. Biro Kratt has insisted that the correct way of doing this is to use the Taylor series for $e^x$.

Your mission, and you have no choice about whether or not to accept it, is to write a FORTRAN program which reads a value from the user and evaluates the function $\exp(\cdot)$ there. Your program should keep adding successive terms to the intermediate result until the answer no longer changes, i.e., the sum is accurate to machine precision. Recall that

$$e^x = 1 + x + \frac{x^2}{2} + \frac{x^3}{6} + \dots + \frac{x^n}{n!} + \dots$$

The program should output the computed value, the number input by the user, the actual value of the function there (obtained by using FORTRAN's EXP function), the absolute error, the relative error, and the number of terms that had to be added. Run the program for the following values of $x$: 1, 5, 10, 15, 20, 25, 30, $-1$, $-5$, $-10$, $-15$, $-20$, and $-30$.

At this point, you should notice that something terrible has happened. Explain what's gone wrong to your boss (by writing down the explanation and handing it in). The future of your job with ACME depends upon your being able to convince your boss that it was his method, rather than your faulty programming, which caused the travesty. If there is a way to correct this problem without abandoning the Taylor series idea, explain what it is. You might be inspired by the equation

$$e^x = \frac{1}{e^{-x}}.$$

Hand in a listing of the program, as well as the output for the values given above, and the explanation for the failure.

**Hint 1:** You should beware that $n!$ is likely to cause an overflow even for moderate values of $n$. This means that you are going to have to make use of the equation

$$\frac{x^n}{n!} = \left(\frac{x^{n-1}}{(n-1)!}\right)\left(\frac{x}{n}\right)$$

in your program.

# Project 3

One division of ACME, the Heuristic Algorithm and Copious Kilobyte Exchange Regulatory agency, is currently designing a package of subroutines for one of ACME's new computer systems. The system, Super-powered Laserized Industrial Development Engine for Rapid, Useful, Logarithmic Encryption, is intended primarily as a supercomputer for numerical computation. The SLIDE RULE should be a revolutionary new tool with which difficult numerical problems might be solved. The HACKER agency is short-handed at the moment, and they are going to need help to complete the programming of the subroutine package. Since SOLVE is not terribly busy at present, many of its consultants are being assigned to HACKER to finish the job. Since you are relatively new to ACME, you have drawn this particular task as your current project.

Your individual task is a relatively straightforward one. Your job is to write a subroutine which solves quadratic equations. In particular, you are supposed to write a FORTRAN subroutine with the following calling sequence:

`SUBROUTINE QUADEQ (A, B, C, R1, R2)`

where the parameters A, B, and C correspond to the coefficients of the equation

$$ax^2 + bx + c = 0,$$

and the parameters R1 and R2 correspond to the two roots of the equation. Your routine should return the real part of the roots if the equation has complex roots.

Since there is an explicit formula for the solution of quadratic equations, namely the quadratic formula

$$r_1 = \frac{-b - \sqrt{b^2 - 4ac}}{2a}, \quad r_2 = \frac{-b + \sqrt{b^2 - 4ac}}{2a},$$

you have what seems like a simple task in front of you. However, your numerical methods experience at BIT makes you skeptical that this problem is as easy as it appears. In particular, you should be aware that you are writing what is often called a *black box*, i.e. a tool which others may come to rely on heavily and which is expected to work all of the time. It is the reliability issue which makes this assignment more than trivial. In particular, your subroutine should work correctly for the following sets of data:

$(i)$     $a = 10^{35}, \quad b = -2 \times 10^{35}, \quad c = 10^{35}$

$(ii)$     $a = 10^{-35}, \quad b = -4 \times 10^{-35}, \quad c = 3 \times 10^{-35}$

$(iii)$     $a = 1, \quad b = -10^{5}, \quad c = 0.25$

$(iv)$     $a = 3.99999, \quad b = -4, \quad c = 1$

$(v)$     $a = 1, \quad b = 0, \quad c = 1$

Once you have finished writing and testing your well-documented subroutine, you should hand in a listing of the subroutine, results of the five tests above, and a report describing what you did to make the results come out right. You may find the following hints helpful:

**Hint 1:** The solutions to the equation $ax^2 + bx + c = 0$ are the same as the solutions to the equation $asx^2 + bsx + cs = 0$ for some non-zero number $s$. This fact may be of some importance.

**Hint 2:** The quadratic formula is unstable if $b^2 \gg 4ac$. Use an alternate formula whenever this is the case.

**Hint 3:** If $b^2 \approx 4ac$, then catastrophic cancellation may occur. To avoid this problem, convert $b^2$ and $4ac$ to double precision, compute the difference, and convert back to single precision. The FORTRAN function DBLE can be used for this purpose.

# Project 4

Because of his newly found confidence in your ability, Biro Kratt has just assigned you to a more challenging project. It appears that the ACME Super Power Usefully Transmitting Nice Information Komputer satellite has begun to malfunction. Your boss swears that it's the last piece of high-tech equipment he will ever buy at a rummage sale. However, the malfunction may still be dealt with, and you have been assigned the task of overcoming the difficulty.

The nature of the malfunction is that 80 per cent of the signal is getting lost in static. Your job is to try to reconstruct the signal based on the 20 per cent of the signal which is getting through. You will attempt to do this using interpolation. In the table below, a part of SPUTNIK's signal has been transcribed. Write a program in FORTRAN which reads in this information, constructs the divided difference table, and then produces a table of signal values spaced at 0.1 second intervals. The signal values should be derived by using cubic (degree 3) polynomial interpolation. Because there are many more function values than 4, you will have to store the full divided difference table in your program. In addition, you will have to make an appropriate choice of interpolating points when you do interpolation.

| TIME | SIGNAL |
|------|--------|
| 0.0 | 1.0000 |
| 0.5 | 2.9950 |
| 1.0 | 3.9801 |
| 1.5 | 4.9553 |
| 2.0 | 5.9211 |
| 2.5 | 6.8776 |
| 3.0 | 7.8253 |
| 3.5 | 8.7648 |
| 4.0 | 9.6967 |
| 4.5 | 10.6216 |
| 5.0 | 11.5403 |

Fortunately, the designer of SPUTNIK was available for consultation, and SOLVE was able to learn that the maximum value of the 4-th derivative of the signal is 0.0016.  Given this information, what is the maximum relative error possible at each of the interpolation points?

You should hand in a listing of your program as well as a table of values from 0 to 5 spaced at 0.1 second intervals. The table should include maximum relative error estimates at each of these points as well. Explain to your boss (in writing) how your program works and how reliable you think your reconstructed signal really is. Because he is going to have to pay your computer bill, be sure to make your program efficient, since the project is already over budget, and you have been informed that computing cost overruns are going to come out of your salary. In particular, be sure to compute the divided difference table only once!

# Project 5

---

ACME has a problem. Wile E. Coyote, one of ACME's best clients for many years, is having trouble with his Locational Operative Responsive Avian Network unit, built by ACME to use radar to track down desert fowl. The LORAN unit provides enough information for most applications, but not for the application which Wile E. Coyote has in mind. The target he would most like to watch moves more quickly than the LORAN unit was designed to handle. Thus, he needs roughly ten times as much data transmitted in any given time period as he is currently getting.

Because ACME needs to keep Wile E. Coyote as a customer, and because the management would rather not shell out the money to design a much improved LORAN unit, you have suggested to your boss that interpolation might solve the problem. In particular, you have agreed to help Wile E. Coyote obtain the necessary data to catch the desert bird he is after. If you are successful, ACME will retain Wile E. Coyote's business. If you fail, then he will almost certainly transfer his business to ACME's chief competitor, AJAX.

The ACME LORAN device transmits a number every 0.2 second. In one typical transmission, the following information was relayed over a two second period of time:

| TIME | DATA |
|------|------|
| 0.0 | 20.0000 |
| 0.2 | 20.6013 |
| 0.4 | 19.6930 |
| 0.6 | 17.5761 |
| 0.8 | 14.7295 |
| 1.0 | 11.7288 |
| 1.2 | 9.1503 |
| 1.4 | 7.4759 |
| 1.6 | 7.0141 |
| 1.8 | 7.8493 |
| 2.0 | 9.8286 |

Your job is going to be to take this data and interpolate it to provide a table of values every 0.02 second. Do this by writing a FORTRAN program which computes the quartic, i.e. degree 4, interpolant to the data above, and evaluates that interpolant at the desired point. Since there are more than 5 points in the table, you are going to have to decide which points to use to construct the interpolating polynomial. Make this decision by using Harten's method, described in one of the hints below.

Your program should construct the first five columns of the divided difference table for the above data. With this table, it should evaluate the appropriate interpolating polynomial, estimating the absolute as well as relative error in the interpolant at each point. The LORAN's principle engineer, a retired ACME employee, has been called for consultation, and from him it has been learned that the absolute value of the 5-th derivative of the signal transmitted by LORAN is bounded by 316. You may or may not find that this information is useful.

Hand in to your boss, who always seems to be interested in how you spend your time at the office, a report containing a listing of your program, the output obtained, your error estimates, and, perhaps most importantly, a written explanation of what you did and why you obtained the results that you did. Your boss, satisfied with your last project, is expecting even better work from you this time. Good luck!

**Hint 1:** Harten's method is a method of choosing appropriate points at which to interpolate. Start with the point $x$ at which the value of the interpolant is desired. Find the interval $[x_i, x_{i+1}]$ containing $x$. Now find the next interpolation point by computing

$$|f[x_{i-1}, x_i, x_{i+1}](x - x_{i-1})|$$

and

$$|f[x_i, x_{i+1}, x_{i+2}](x - x_{i+2})|.$$

If the first quantity is smaller, add $x_{i-1}$. If the second quantity is smaller, add $x_{i+2}$. In general, to add a point to $x_i, ..., x_j$, compute

$$|f[x_{i-1}, x_i, ..., x_j](x - x_{i-1})|$$

and

$$|f[x_i, ..., x_j, x_{j+1}](x - x_{j+1})|.$$

Add either $x_{i-1}$ or $x_{j+1}$ to the list of points, whichever corresponds to the smaller computed value. Keep adding points in this way until the proper number of points have been added.

**Hint 2:** Write a generic program. Do not write a program which depends specifically upon the data given above. A non-generic program will be less useful, and harder to write anyway.

# Project 6

Research teams from the Group for Organizing Treks to Logically Omitted Special Terrain are currently planning expeditions to the South Pole and the Sahara Desert. GOT LOST has decided to buy ACME tricorders to take along as research tools.

Like most of ACME's other electronic gadgets, the tricorder is a collection of various microchips, wired together in some fashion to produce (with any luck) a useful device. Because of the nature of the $pn$ junctions in the transistors, the relationship between voltage and current in this circuitry satisfies the ideal diode equation:

$$i = I_S(T)\left(e^{qv/kT} - 1\right).$$

Here $i$ is the current, $q$ is the charge of an electron ($1.6 \times 10^{-19}$ coulomb), $v$ is the voltage, $k$ is Boltzmann's constant ($1.38 \times 10^{-23}$ joule/degree Kelvin), and $T$ is the temperature on the Kelvin scale (centigrade temperature $+273.16$). $I_S(T)$ is the saturation current, a function of temperature as well as the doping of the chips in their manufacture process. Because ACME has cut costs as much as possible, all of the circuitry in the tricorders is made up of chips whose saturation current function is

$$I_S(T) = i_s e^{-\left(\frac{R-T}{10}\right)^2},$$

where $i_s$ is a doping constant ($10^{-13}$ ampere) and $R$ is room temperature (293.16 K).

Because of the extreme temperatures in the places GOT LOST is going, ACME has asked you to determine the working temperature range of its tricorders. In one part of the circuitry, there is always at least a 1 volt potential difference across a critical transistor, which must always have at least a 1 ampere current running through it for the tricorder to function.

Your job is to write a FORTRAN program to solve for the two critical temperatures at which the current is exactly 1 amp. It is known that between the two temperatures the device will function correctly, but will fail to work at all outside this range. Use Newton's method to solve this problem, and print results in degrees Fahrenheit. Bear in mind that the equations are only valid for temperatures given on the Kelvin scale. You may have to play around a bit to get starting guesses which will converge to each of the two critical temperatures.

As usual, hand in a listing of your program, its output, and a written explanation of your findings.

# Project 7

The Corporate Headquarters for Extraneous Accounting Procedures, an administrative group within ACME, needs to make an important business decision. CHEAP wants to borrow $100 million in order to finance an important research project whose ultimate success will prove extremely beneficial for ACME. CHEAP has located two potential sources for this money. The first, Mutual United Stock and Corporate Liabilities Exchange, is willing to loan the $100 million at an annual interest rate which has not yet been negotiated. CHEAP would be expected to repay the loan over 10 years by making ten equal payments to MUSCLE at the end of each year. The other source of money is the Security Home Annuity Refund Kartel. SHARK is willing to loan the money to CHEAP at 13 per cent annual interest. However, SHARK wishes to be paid only the $13 million in interest at the end of each year for ten years, followed by the repayment of the entire $100 million at the end of the tenth year. In order to have the $100 million available at the end of ten years with which to repay the loan, under SHARK's arrangement, it will be necessary to set up a sinking fund. A sinking fund may be thought of as a kind of annuity, or savings account, to which equal payments are made for a certain amount of time and then the whole balance is paid to a second party, in this case SHARK. In CHEAP's case, it is possible to set up a sinking fund which can earn 10 per cent annual interest.

In any event, the negotiators at CHEAP would like to know what interest rate MUSCLE needs to agree to in order to provide an equivalent deal to that offered by SHARK. Your boss has agreed that this kind of computation should be right up your alley, and he has volunteered your services for this project. Your computation has the potential of saving ACME millions of dollars in interest payments, so it is very important.

The relevant information for this project is contained in the following equations. To compute the payment on a loan, you should use the formula:

$$p = \frac{iA(1+i)^n}{(1+i)^n - 1},$$

where $i$ is the interest rate, $A$ is the amount of the loan, $n$ is the number of payments which need to be made, and $p$ is the amount of each payment. A sinking fund or annuity is governed by the equation

$$p = \frac{iS}{(1+i)^n - 1},$$

where $i$ is the interest rate, $S$ is the amount of the sinking fund or annuity, $n$ is the number of payments made into the sinking fund or annuity, and $p$ is the amount of each payment. These equations can be easily derived by considering how loans and savings accounts work and then simplifying the resulting geometric series.

You should write a concise FORTRAN program to carry out this computation. In addition to a listing of your program, you should hand in a report describing your computation, and a conditional recommendation to CHEAP detailing which offer you would choose depending upon the final interest rate which is negotiated with MUSCLE.

**Hint 1:** Use the NAG routine C05ADF. It will help you compute interest rates. You will need to use a FORTRAN COMMON statement.

**Hint 2:** Assume that all interest is compounded annually.

**Hint 3:** Write a general program. A specific program will get the job done, but it only works for the given problem and tends to be harder to debug than one which is more general. Try to make things like interest rates, principles, number of payments, etc. variable within the program.

# Project 8

Based on your past successes, Biro Kratt has recommended that you assist on a project of great importance to ACME. The Republic United Steel Truss division of ACME manufactured steel beams for a customer, Monolithic Engineering Steel Structures. These beams were used in the construction of a structure called the Unduly Gigantic Hanger. Several of the UGHs have shown signs of severe fatigue, and MESS is suing ACME, claiming that the beams produced by RUST are at fault. RUST maintains that the beams were made to specifications and believes that UGH is so constructed that the beams are subjected to forces beyond specifications. Your task is to analyze UGH to determine the forces to which the beams are subjected.

The UGH is constructed with twenty seven (27) beams, or members, connected at eleven (11) joints. MESS has specified that each beam is required to withstand extension forces of up to 20 tons and compressive forces up to 17 tons without fatigue failure. Through a court order, ACME has obtained from MESS the data on the UGH. The figure shows what the UGH looks like. The loads are attached to joint 11.

The specifications for the UGH are contained in the following tables. The first table contains the coordinates of the joints. For example, joint 3 is at the point $(6.5, -2.15, 0.0)$ relative to the origin, which is joint 1.

| JOINT | x | y | z |
|-------|-------|-------|------|
| 1 | 0.00 | 0.00 | 0.00 |
| 2 | 6.50 | 2.15 | 0.00 |
| 3 | 6.50 | −2.15 | 0.00 |
| 4 | −1.00 | 0.00 | 5.54 |
| 5 | 4.10 | 1.63 | 5.54 |
| 6 | 4.10 | −1.63 | 5.54 |
| 7 | 7.20 | 3.26 | 5.54 |
| 8 | 7.20 | 0.00 | 5.54 |
| 9 | 7.20 | −3.26 | 5.54 |
| 10 | 0.50 | 0.00 | 7.83 |
| 11 | 9.86 | 0.00 | 6.54 |

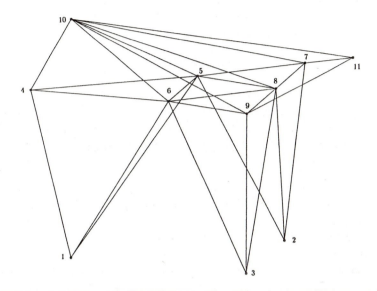

The second table contains the connection information, which in this case is given by a number of beams, together with the two joints they connect, e.g. beam 3 connects joint 1 and joint 6:

| BEAM | JOINT 1 | JOINT 2 | BEAM | JOINT 1 | JOINT 2 |
|---|---|---|---|---|---|
| 1 | 1 | 4 | 15 | 5 | 8 |
| 2 | 1 | 5 | 16 | 6 | 8 |
| 3 | 1 | 6 | 17 | 8 | 9 |
| 4 | 2 | 5 | 18 | 6 | 9 |
| 5 | 2 | 7 | 19 | 4 | 10 |
| 6 | 2 | 8 | 20 | 5 | 10 |
| 7 | 3 | 8 | 21 | 7 | 10 |
| 8 | 3 | 9 | 22 | 8 | 10 |
| 9 | 3 | 6 | 23 | 9 | 10 |
| 10 | 4 | 5 | 24 | 6 | 10 |
| 11 | 4 | 6 | 25 | 10 | 11 |
| 12 | 5 | 6 | 26 | 7 | 11 |
| 13 | 5 | 7 | 27 | 9 | 11 |
| 14 | 7 | 8 | | | |

To find the forces on each of the beams, use the equations expressing the idea that the forces on the beams at each joint must balance the applied load. The equations can be written out as follows. The equation for the $x$ component of the force at joint number $j$ is

$$\sum f_m \cos(j, k; x) = -\text{load}_{j,x} \tag{1}$$

where the sum is over all beams $m$ which connect to joint $j$ and where $k$ is the joint which is connected to $j$ by $m$. The quantity $f_m$ is the force on beam $m$, which you are to determine, and $\cos(j, k; x)$ is the cosine of the angle between the $x$ direction and the beam connecting joints $j$ and $k$. The direction cosine is computed as

$$\cos(j, k; x) = \frac{(x(k) - x(j))}{\text{dist}(j, k)}, \tag{2}$$

where $\text{dist}(j, k)$ is the distance between joints $j$ and $k$.

The equations for the $y$ and $z$ components of the force are similar to (1) and (2) with the $x$ replaced by $y$ and $z$. These equations give 33 equations, i.e. 3 equations for each of the 11 joints, for the 27 forces on the beams, i.e. the $f_m$. Six equations are eliminated from the system to account for the UGH being secured to the ground. For joint 1 remove the equations for the $y$ and $z$ equations and for both joints 2 and 3 remove the $x$ and $z$ equations. Thus we obtain 27 equations for the 27 unknowns. The load applied to joint 11 has components $(0.0, 1.0, -10.0)$.

You must solve this linear system of equations to determine the forces on UGH given the load on joint 11. Write a computer program which sets up the matrix from the data in the file and then calls the NAG routine F01BTF to factor the matrix into its LU decomposition. Your program must then call the routine F04AYF to obtain the forces. The forces are compression forces if they are negative, and they are extension forces if they are positive. Check to see if the forces on the beams exceed those specified by MESS.

Your program should be somewhat generic in setting up the matrix. However, it need not be general in terms of which equations are eliminated nor in the specification of the load. Write a report showing your conclusions. Include with your report a listing of your program and a display of the output.

**Hint 1:** Beware that $\cos(j, k; x) = -\cos(k, j; x)$.

**Hint 2:** Construct a data file containing the data on the UGH. This will simplify the setting up of the matrix.

# Project 9

A certain division of the company, namely the ACME Team Research Organization Committee for Investigating Oceans and Underwater Stuff, has sent one of its research ships, *S.S. Gaussian Rule*, on a voyage to gather data off the coast of Venezuela. Under orders from ATROCIOUS, *Gaussian Rule* has spent the last few days in the triangular region of ocean whose vertices are at 12° North latitude 65° West longitude, 12° North 64° West, and 13° N. 65° W., just north of Blanquilla Island.

The ship is equipped with (among other things) two different recording devices for measuring oceanographic data. The French Remote Offshore Gauge records subtle differences in pressure at sea level, while the Temperate Offshore Analytic Device records weak shifts in the earth's electromagnetic field. The following data have been collected by the FROG and TOAD aboard *Gaussian Rule*:

| LOCATION | FROG | TOAD |
|---|---|---|
| 12° N. 65° W. | 0.0 | 0.3678795 |
| 12° N. 64°45′ W. | 0.2309699 | 0.3916056 |
| 12° N. 64°30′ W. | 0.3535534 | 0.4723665 |
| 12° N. 64°15′ W. | 0.2870126 | 0.6456485 |
| 12° N. 64° W. | 0.0 | 1.0 |
| 12°15′ N. 65° W. | 0.0956709 | 0.3916056 |
| 12°15′ N. 64°45′ W. | 0.3266408 | 0.4168620 |
| 12°15′ N. 64°30′ W. | 0.4492243 | 0.5028316 |
| 12°15′ N. 64°15′ W. | 0.3826835 | 0.6872893 |
| 12°30′ N. 65° W. | 0.3535534 | 0.4723665 |
| 12°30′ N. 64°45′ W. | 0.5845233 | 0.5028316 |
| 12°30′ N. 64°30′ W. | 0.7071068 | 0.6065307 |
| 12°45′ N. 65° W. | 0.6929097 | 0.6456485 |
| 12°45′ N. 64°45′ W. | 0.9238796 | 0.6872893 |
| 13° N. 65° W. | 1.0 | 1.0 |

ATROCIOUS would like to have some idea of the general behavior of these readings in the triangular patch of sea explored by *Gaussian Rule*. Thus your job will be to construct two interpolating polynomials, one for each set of data. You will have to do this by solving two $15 \times 15$ linear systems of equations. You may assume that the earth is flat in the appropriate region.

Each system will use the same matrix, but a different right hand side. Use NAG routines F01BTF to factor the matrix and F04AYF to solve the systems. Use the interpolants to estimate FROG and TOAD values at $12°20'$ N. $64°40'$ W.

As usual, your boss expects you to hand in a work report describing what you did, a listing of your program, the computed coefficients of your two interpolating polynomials, and your estimated FROG and TOAD readings at the desired location. You may find the following hints helpful:

**Hint 1:** Change the unwieldy latitude and longitude figures into something more convenient. For example, you could let $12°$ N. $65°$ W. be the point $(0,0)$, and let $12°$ N. $64°$ W. be the point $(1,0)$. All other points can be assigned similar coordinates. You may find it helpful to plot the geographic coordinates on a piece of paper and then assign the usual Cartesian coordinates to those points.

**Hint 2:** A general degree 4 polynomial in two variables in given by the formula:

$$p_4(x,y) := a_1 + a_2x + a_3x^2 + a_4x^3 + a_5x^4 + a_6y + a_7xy + a_8x^2y +$$
$$a_9x^3y + a_{10}y^2 + a_{11}xy^2 + a_{12}x^2y^2 + a_{13}y^3 + a_{14}xy^3 + a_{15}y^4$$

This function is completely determined by the 15 coefficients. Since the goal is to compute an interpolating polynomial, the equation

$$p_4(x,y) = f(x,y)$$

must be satisfied at all 15 of the points given in the table. This leads to a linear system of 15 equations with the $a_i$ as unknowns.

**Hint 3:** Writing the code to compute the coefficients of the matrix takes some thought. Do not put this project off until the last minute.

# Project 10

The Superconductor Hotshot Operational Research Team, a division of ACME, has been producing an electronic device, called the Fortified Utility Switching Engine, for the Bureaucratic, Large, Overblown, Washington Network, a branch of the federal government. The SHORT FUSE has been manufactured under strict specifications, which SHORT has supposedly upheld. Recently, however, some of the BLOWN FUSEs have begun to fail, and BLOWN is preparing to cancel its contract with ACME, claiming that the SHORT FUSEs have not been manufactured to specifications.

Naturally, SOLVE has been called in to investigate this matter. Since you have much expertise in this area, you have been selected by Biro Kratt as the individual responsible for discovering just what is going on and who is to blame. The successful completion of this project may well allow SHORT to retain its multimillion-dollar contract with BLOWN. A personal salary increase may also be in the offing if you are successful.

The FUSE is a complicated device, but the problems which BLOWN is having are all located in a small part of the circuitry. This part of the circuitry is displayed in the schematic diagram opposite. The object listed as $V$ is a six volt battery, and the 28 resistors are placed as shown. In addition, with certain options on the FUSE enabled, there may or may not be an auxiliary 1.5 volt battery at $A$. All of the BLOWN FUSEs have been failing at $B$, a sensitive black box which is not designed to handle more than 0.6 ampere of current. In addition, the wiring is delicate enough so that it will melt if the current ever exceeds 0.9 ampere at any point.

BLOWN is claiming that one of the two specifications, and perhaps both, are not being met by SHORT. Thus, you are going to have to solve for the current throughout this device to determine if the current at any point exceeds 0.9 ampere. In addition, you must determine whether the current through $B$ ever exceeds 0.6 ampere. The actual black box placed at $B$ is not manufactured by SHORT, and its circuitry is unknown.

You will solve this problem by using the current loop law. This law says that, for any loop, the sum of the voltages around the loop must be zero. The relationship between the current $i$, the voltage $v$, and the resistance $r$ is $v = ir$. This means that across each resistor there is a voltage drop of $ir$, where $i$ is the current through the resistor. The battery $V$ produces a voltage of six volts, while $A$ may or may not produce 1.5 volts. Each of the

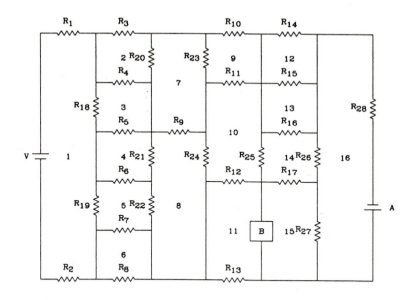

sixteen loops given in the schematic diagram may be considered to have a current flowing around it in the clockwise direction (counter-clockwise if you happen to be right-handed). In addition, currents through wires which are common to two loops may be summed. Thus, the current through $R_{18}$ is given by $i_1 - i_3$, since $i_1$ and $i_3$ are flowing in opposite directions through $R_{18}$. Thus, for each loop, a linear equation may be written involving the variables $i_1$, $i_2$, ..., $i_{16}$, since all of the resistances are known.

Your job will be to write a FORTRAN program to solve two linear systems, corresponding to the cases when a 1.5 volt battery is absent or present at $A$. Thus, your program must construct a $16 \times 16$ matrix and two 16 component vectors. This done, it should call the NAG routines F01BTF and F04AYF to solve the linear systems. Each subroutine should only be called once!

The resistors given in the diagram have the following values: $R_1$ is a $4\Omega$ (ohm) resistor, $R_2$, $R_4$, $R_5$, $R_7$, $R_9$, $R_{10}$, $R_{11}$, $R_{12}$, $R_{14}$, $R_{18}$, $R_{19}$, $R_{20}$, $R_{25}$, $R_{26}$, and $R_{27}$ are $2\Omega$ resistors, and all of the rest are $1\Omega$ resistors.

Write up a detailed project summary describing your program, the method used, and the results of your computation. In particular, try to determine if SHORT has not built the FUSE to specifications. If not, then determine who is responsible for causing the FUSE to fail. It is not your job to acquit SHORT; it is your job to discover the truth and report it.

**Hint 1:** You may find it very helpful to construct a file which contains the value of a resistor and the loops to which it belongs. For example, construct a file of 28 lines, each line of which contains $j$, $R_j$, $k$, and $\ell$, where $j$ is the number of the resistor, $R_j$ is the resistance of the resistor, and $k$ and $\ell$ are the two loops to which $j$ belongs. Then, by reading this file, it is possible to construct the matrix needed for the problem in a straightforward manner.

**Hint 2:** Most of the entries for the right-hand side vector for the problems should be zero.

**Hint 3:** In Hint 1, if a resistor only belongs to one loop, then set $\ell$ to zero.

# Project 11

The Mechanical Operations Utility Staff for Engineering Technology for Research And Production, a division of ACME, is currently designing a new motor to be used in many of its products. The old motor is large, heavy, and relatively energy inefficient by modern standards, so ACME has decided to invest in the development of an improved motor to improve the quality of the products. Thus, many of the division's employees are currently working on this project in order to build a better MOUSETRAP motor.

In any case, the new MOUSETRAP motor project is well underway. In fact, a prototype is already functioning in the lab. However, the testing of this new motor is far from complete. One of the current projects is to determine the startup response of the motor. The MOUSETRAP lab has already made several measurements, but they do not yet have a good mathematical model of what is going on. They have asked SOLVE for assistance, and this assignment has landed in your lap. Being the helpful individual that you are, you have happily agreed to solve this problem.

Essentially the measurements have been obtained in a straightforward manner. The new motor is attached to a spool of threadlike material to which a small piece of reflective material has been attached at a certain point. The spool of thread is gently unwound and laid along a table top in a straight line away from the spool. This piece of material is aligned with a marking on the table. There are further markings on the table placed at 1 millimeter intervals. The motor is started at time $t = 0$. The running motor winds up the thread onto the spool. This causes the piece of reflective material on the thread to pass successive table markings. As each mark is passed, the time is recorded. In one such experiment, the following data were collected:

| TIME (milliseconds) | DISTANCE |
|---|---|
| 0.00 | 0.0 |
| 1.40 | 1.0 |
| 2.37 | 2.0 |
| 3.30 | 3.0 |
| 3.37 | 4.0 |

Mehra, R., and E. Prescott. 1985. "The Equity Premium: a Puzzle." *Journal of Monetary Economics* 15: 145–61.

Merton, R. C. 1973. "An Intertemporal Capital Asset Pricing Model." *Econometrica* 41: 867–88.

———. 1980. "On Estimating the Expected Return on the Market: an Exploratory Investigation." *Journal of Financial Economics* 8: 323–61.

Mossin, J. 1966. "Equilibrium in a Capital Asset Market." *Econometrica* 34: 768–83.

Muth, J. F. 1961. "Rational Expectations and the Theory of Price Movements." *Econometrica* 29: 315–35.

Negishi, T. 1962. "The Stability of the Competitive Equilibrium. A Survey Article." *Econometrica* 30: 635–70.

Rabin, M. 2000. "Risk Aversion and Expected-Utility Theory: a Calibration Theorem." *Econometrica* 68: 1281–92.

Radner, R. 1972. "Existence of Equilibrium of Plans, Prices, and Price Expectations in a Sequence of Markets." *Econometrica* 40: 289–303.

Ritter, J. R. 1991. "The Long-Run Performance of Initial Public Offerings." *Journal of Finance* 46: 3–28.

Roll, R. 1977. "A Critique of the Asset Pricing Theory's Tests, Part I: on the Past and Potential Testability of the Theory." *Journal of Financial Economics* 4: 129–76.

Ross, S. 1978. "Mutual Fund Separation in Financial Theory—the Separating Distributions." *Journal of Economic Theory* 17: 254–86.

Rubinstein, M. 1974. "An Aggregation Theorem for Securities Markets." *Journal of Financial Economics* 1: 225–44.

———. 1976. "The Valuation of Uncertain Income Streams and the Pricing of Options." *The Bell Journal of Economics* 7: 407–25.

Sharpe, W. 1964. "Capital Asset Prices: a Theory of Market Equilibrium under Conditions of Risk." *Journal of Finance* 19: 425–42.

Stambaugh, R. 1982. "On the Exclusion of Assets from Tests of the Two-Parameter Model: a Sensitivity Analysis." *Journal of Financial Economics* 10: 237–68.

Stapleton, R., and M. Subrahmanyam. 1978. "A Multiperiod Equilibrium Asset Pricing Model." *Econometrica* 46: 1077–93.

Sundaresan, S. 1989. "Intertemporally Dependent Preferences and the Volatility of Consumption and Wealth." *Review of Financial Studies* 2: 73–89.

Wohl, A., and S. Kandel. 1997. "Implications of an Index-Contingent Trading Mechanism." *Journal of Business* 70: 471–88.

| TIME (milliseconds) | DISTANCE |
|:---:|:---:|
| 4.11 | 5.0 |
| 5.42 | 6.0 |
| 5.71 | 7.0 |
| 6.39 | 8.0 |
| 7.26 | 9.0 |
| 7.82 | 10.0 |
| 8.67 | 11.0 |
| 9.12 | 12.0 |
| 9.66 | 13.0 |
| 10.70 | 14.0 |
| 11.23 | 15.0 |
| 11.25 | 16.0 |
| 12.47 | 17.0 |
| 12.79 | 18.0 |
| 13.20 | 19.0 |
| 14.12 | 20.0 |
| 14.83 | 21.0 |
| 15.83 | 22.0 |
| 16.04 | 23.0 |

The lab technicians at MOUSETRAP admit to not using terribly precise instruments, so many of these numbers are likely to be in error. You have decided to model this as a quartic (degree 4) polynomial. Since there are many more measurements than can possibly be satisfied by a simple quartic polynomial, you are going to have to use some sort of least-squares approach to solve the problem.

In order to complete this project, you are going to have to write a FORTRAN program which takes the above data, constructs the appropriate polynomial from it, and then produces a graph of the resulting function. Hand in to your boss a listing of the program, the graph, and a written report of everything that you had to do in order to obtain it. You should pay strict attention to the following hint, or your boss may get quite upset.

**Hint 1:** The matrix that you will set up for this problem is an overdetermined **Vandermonde** matrix. Since the Vandermonde is often ill-conditioned, solving the normal equations in order to compute the least-squares answer to the problem is a terrible thing to do. The QR decomposition is a much better idea. Use the NAG routine F04JGF.

# Project 12

---

ACME's new Humble Automatic Lackey 9000, an industrial robot (also mentioned in Project 1), has not been as reliable as the competition's robot, i.e. AJAX's Newfangled Electronic Robotic Device. The main difficulty is that the arm movement is not smooth and this has placed undue strain on the various joints and mechanisms. Because of your reputation as a trouble-shooter you have been asked to investigate this problem.

The robot arm consists of four sections with lengths $L_1$, $L_2$, $L_3$, and $L_4$. The direction of each section of the arm is specified by the unit vectors

$$v_m = (c_{1,m}, c_{2,m}, c_{3,m})$$

which point in the direction of the $m^{th}$ section. The direction cosine $c_{i,m}$ is the cosine of the angle between the $m^{th}$ member and the $i^{th}$ coordinate direction. Thus the equations for the location of the far end of the fourth member are

$$x_i = \sum_{m=1}^{4} L_m c_{i,m}, \qquad i = 1, 2, 3, \tag{1}$$

relative to the origin, which is the beginning of the first section. The direction cosines satisfy

$$c_{1,m}^2 + c_{2,m}^2 + c_{3,m}^2 = 1 \tag{2}$$

since the direction vectors are unit vectors. To move the end of the arm a small amount $(\Delta x_1, \Delta x_2, \Delta x_3)$, the changes to the direction cosines must be determined. The equation governing the arm movement is

$$\sum_{m=1}^{4} L_m \Delta c_{i,m} = \Delta x_i, \qquad i = 1, 2, 3. \tag{3}$$

The changes in the direction cosines, $\Delta c_{i,m}$, are not arbitrary but must be constrained to keep the direction vectors of unit length. This constraint is expressed in the equation

$$c_{1,m} \Delta c_{1,m} + c_{2,m} \Delta c_{2,m} + c_{3,m} \Delta c_{3,m} = 0, \qquad m = 1, 2, 3, 4. \tag{4}$$

There are therefore 7 equations, i.e. (3) and (4), for the 12 unknowns given by the $\Delta c_{i,m}$. That there are more unknowns than equations is not surprising because there are usually many ways to configure HAL's arm to have its end at a given point. Since the number of equations is not equal to the number of unknowns, this problem is a natural candidate for an application of the singular value decomposition.

To move HAL's arm from a starting point $x_s = (x_{1,s}, x_{2,s}, x_{3,s})$ toward a final point $x_f = (x_{1,f}, x_{2,f}, x_{3,f})$, set $\Delta x$ to be a multiple of the unit vector from $x_s$ to $x_f$. That is, the change in $x$ should be no more than some tolerance in magnitude and in the direction of $x_f - x_s$. (See hint 4 for information on the tolerances.) This determines the right-hand side for the linear system. After setting up the matrix for this system of equations, use the NAG routine F02WAF to compute the singular value decomposition of the matrix, and then transform the system to the standard form

$$\Sigma V^T \Delta c \approx U^T \Delta x. \tag{5}$$

Obtain a reasonable solution of equation (5) and compute the values of the $\Delta c_{i,m}$ and update the direction cosines. Note that the vectors resulting from adding the solution of the linear system to the direction cosine unit vector need not satisfy equation (2). You must renormalize these new vectors to be unit vectors.

After the arm has been moved to a new position, i.e. a new $x_s$ has been determined, then the process is repeated to determine the next change of position.

To be certain that the movement of the arm is smooth you must ensure that the change in the direction cosines is small. Thus if you obtain a quantity of large magnitude when you divide by the singular values, you should reset it to have the magnitude $tol_c$ and with the same sign as before.

When your program is ready to go, apply it to the following series of six tests for HAL to go through. Each test is described by a $5 \times 3$ matrix. The first four rows of each matrix give the direction cosines for the starting position. The last row contains the coordinates of the final position:

|  |  |  |  |  |  |  |  |  |
|---|---|---|---|---|---|---|---|---|
| 1.0 | 0.0 | 0.0 | 1.0 | 0.0 | 0.0 | 1.0 | 0.0 | 0.0 |
| 0.0 | 1.0 | 0.0 | 0.6 | 0.8 | 0.0 | 0.0 | 1.0 | 0.0 |
| 0.0 | 1.0 | 0.0 | 0.0 | 1.0 | 0.0 | 0.0 | 0.8 | 0.6 |
| 0.0 | 0.0 | 1.0 | 0.0 | 0.0 | 1.0 | 0.0 | 0.0 | 1.0 |
| 6.0 | 3.0 | 1.0 | −1.0 | −1.0 | −1.0 | 0.2 | 0.3 | 0.3 |
|  |  |  |  |  |  |  |  |  |
| 1.0 | 0.0 | 0.0 | 1.0 | 0.0 | 0.0 | −1.0 | 0.0 | 0.0 |
| 0.0 | 1.0 | 0.0 | 0.0 | 1.0 | 0.0 | 1.0 | 0.0 | 0.0 |
| 1.0 | 0.0 | 0.0 | 0.0 | 1.0 | 0.0 | −1.0 | 0.0 | 0.0 |
| 0.0 | 0.0 | 1.0 | 0.0 | 0.0 | 1.0 | 1.0 | 0.0 | 0.0 |
| −0.2 | −1.0 | −0.3 | −0.2 | −1.0 | −0.3 | −1.0 | 0.0 | 0.0 |

The lengths of HAL's arm sections are given by:

$$L_1 = 1.0 \qquad L_2 = 4.0 \qquad L_3 = 1.0 \qquad L_4 = 1.5$$

**Hint 1:** There is a limit on how far HAL can reach and also a limit on how close to the origin HAL can reach. Your program should check that the final position is reachable by HAL.

**Hint 2:** In some configurations of the arm the matrix will have small singular values. Only divide by a singular value if it is larger than some tolerance. See Hint 4.

**Hint 3:** There is the possibility that the arm will lock up. This occurs when all the arm sections lie on a line and the final position is also on that line. This is detected when there is no solution to the linear system and the changes to the direction vectors as determined by your SVD procedure are parallel to the direction vectors themselves. In this situation you must devise some way to move the arm, but only a little bit, so the sections are not all on the same line. You can check for a locked arm by considering the quantity

$$\sum_{m=1}^{4} |v_m \cdot \Delta v_m| / \|\Delta v_m\|.$$

When this quantity is 4.0 then the arm is locked. (Why?)

**Hint 4:** Choose the tolerances so that the maximum value of $\Delta x_i$ and the changes in the direction cosine vectors, $\|v_m\|$, are less than 0.10 over the course of the movement.

**Hint 5:** For your report on this project hand in a written discussion of what you did and a listing of your well documented program. Also, for each of the test cases, show how many steps your program took to go from the starting position to the final position, and show that the arm motion is relatively smooth by producing estimates for the maximum changes in the coordinates and the maximum changes in the direction cosines per step over the course of the movement.

**Hint 6:** The NAG routine F02WAF only works for systems with at least as many rows as columns. This means that you are going to have to pad your system with rows of zeroes (or replicate one of the other rows). Alternatively, you may use the routine F02WCF from the NAG FORTRAN Library if it is available.

# Project 13

A fresh supply of crude melange has just been delivered from the planet Arrakis. Melange is a valuable spice with fantastic properties; it is known to slow the ageing process by a factor of nearly four, and those who take it in heavy doses are sometimes capable of seeing the future. In any case, the Production of Chemical Brilliance division of ACME has a contract with the Nutritional Union of the True Monarchy of Extraterrestrial Galaxies to refine the crude melange into a more pure form. To do this, the PCB division has designed a machine for NUTMEG which does the refining.

This machine has a hopper which is initially loaded with 100 kg of crude spice. The machine is turned on and allowed to run. It starts producing pure melange at the rate of 1 kg/minute. However, this rate begins to fall off quickly, for the concentration of spice in the hopper decreases as more and more pure melange is removed. Suppose that the rate at which pure spice comes out of the machine is given as a function of time, say $R(t)$. The designers of the machine know that $R(t)$ satisfies the differential equation:

$$R'(t) = -\frac{R(t)}{10(R(t) + 1)}, \qquad R(0) = 1 \text{ kg/minute.}$$

As it turns out, the solution to this differential equation is given by the relation

$$R(t)e^{R(t)} = e^{1-t/10}.$$

This relation is **implicit**, which means that one does not have an explicit formula for computing $R(t)$ when given a value for $t$.

The accounting department at ACME is very interested in knowing how much pure melange can be produced in one hour by this machine, since it is important to them to know something about the cost effectiveness of this process. Your boss, his confidence in your ability growing with every successful project you work on, has volunteered your services. It will be your job to compute this number.

As usual, you will write a FORTRAN program to do the computation. Your program should call the NAG routine D01AJF to do the actual numerical integration. Use a relative error tolerance of $10^{-5}$ when you call D01AJF. Turn in a listing of the program, the number of kilograms the machine can produce in an hour, and an explanation of what you did in your computation.

**Hint 1:** You will find the NAG routine C05ADF useful.

# Project 14

---

The Medical And Legal Professions' Research Associates for Computerized Technical and Industrial Complex Enzymes, a division of ACME which develops and manufactures medical products, has just come out with a new wonder drug, *cramerrulic*, used for treating cancer patients. It does a terrific job of controlling the growth of many kinds of malignant tumors, but it has a very undesirable side effect: even in moderate doses, it has a tendency to kill the patient. The drug has not yet been approved by the FDA, but MALPRACTICE has received permission to prescribe it to patients whose chances of survival are almost non-existent without it.

One of these patients, suffering from a deadly form of cancer known as *instability sarcoma*, is currently in surgery. *Instability sarcoma* is related to the much less dangerous, but somewhat better studied, cancer known as *roundoff sarcoma*. Since the tumor in the patient is known to be inoperable in the sense that all of it cannot be removed, MALPRACTICE intends to use *cramerrulic* to attempt to keep the growth of the tumor under control. However, prescribing just the right amount of *cramerrulic* to control the tumor without killing the patient is going to require a tricky computation. MALPRACTICE has asked your boss at ACME for assistance, and because there are lives at stake, he has insisted on sending his best consultant to do the job. The patient's life is now in your hands.

*Instability sarcoma* produces tumors whose growth rates satisfy the following differential equation:

$$r'(t) = \frac{-\alpha r(t)^2}{1 + \alpha r(t)t} \tag{1}$$

where $r(t)$ is the rate (in grams per day) at which the tumor grows, $t$ is the time (in days), and $\alpha$ is the number of milligrams of *cramerrulic* which the patient consumes each day. Notice that the rate of growth is constant in the absence of *cramerrulic*, but slows down significantly in the presense of the drug. The solution to this differential equation is given by the following equation (the initial condition is a consequence of the surgery currently being performed):

$$r(t) = e^{4-\alpha r(t)t}. \tag{2}$$

The first 36 hours following the surgery are going to be critical. During that time, it is essential that the size of the tumor be kept smaller than 6 grams. If it exceeds this size, it will impinge on the brain tissue surrounding it, causing the patient's involuntary nervous system to fail, resulting in her death. The mass of the tumor (in grams) is given by the following equation:

$$M(t) = 0.75 + \int_0^t r(s)\mathrm{d}s. \tag{3}$$

The expected mass of the tumor following surgery is expected to be 0.75 grams, which is why that number appears in this equation. This mass must depend upon $\alpha$, since $r(t)$ depends upon $\alpha$ in an essential way.

Your job is to compute the minimum dosage of *cramerrulic* which will keep the size of the tumor at 6 grams or less during the first 36 hours following surgery. With any luck, this will be an amount small enough to avoid poisoning the patient. You will do this by writing a FORTRAN program which uses the secant method to solve equation (3) for the appropriate value of $\alpha$. Bear in mind that even 5 milligrams of *cramerrulic* a day are enough to kill a normal human being.

Once you have computed the proper dosage, write a report explaining how you solved the problem and why you believe your answer is correct. Turn in (to your boss at ACME) a listing of your well-structured FOR-TRAN program (which must make use of the NAG FORTRAN Library in an essential way), the report explaining what you did, and your prognosis of the patient's chances for survival. You may find the following hints helpful in preparing your prescription:

**Hint 1:** The NAG routines C05ADF and D01AJF will be extremely useful. However, because FORTRAN routines cannot call themselves (either directly or indirectly), C05ADF should not be used to compute the value of $\alpha$ directly. Use the secant method to compute $\alpha$.

**Hint 2:** Parameter passing for this problem is quite tricky. The best way of getting around this problem is to use the FORTRAN COMMON statement.

**Hint 3:** Your program should only be about 40 lines long (not counting the many comments which you will include).

# Project 15

The Board of Engineers for Aqueous Voluminous Edifices and Restraints, the civil engineering division of ACME, is currently working on the design for a dam to be constructed in the Oscillating Gorge on the Interpolant River, not far from the town of Runge's Mill. Recently, however, an environmentalist group, the Demagogues Against Mutilating Nature, have begun to protest against the construction of the Oscillating Gorge Dam. The DAMN outcry 'Stop the damn dam' has been so successful, in fact, that ACME has been served with a court injunction preventing the start of the actual construction. In order for BEAVER to continue work on its dam, ACME is going to have to get DAMN satisfied.

The environmental impact of the dam is a complex issue, especially because the flow rate of the Interpolant River is so variable. One of the problems in answering the DAMN concerns is that no one is really quite sure what the hydrostatic pressure behind the dam is going to be as a function of the height of the water. Because the flow rate is so variable, the dam is going to have to be built in order to withstand greatly varying pressures. In order for the engineers to submit an acceptable design, it is going to be necessary to know just what those pressures are. This is where you come in. You are going to have to determine the hydrostatic pressure. Biro Kratt has assigned you to this project because of your reputation for integrity, knowing that DAMN will abide by your findings.

The dam that BEAVER wants to build is 100 feet high. It is only 20 feet wide at the bottom, and $x$ feet above the bottom, the width of the dam is given by

$$w = 40 - 20e^{-(0.01x)^2} \text{ feet.}$$

Suppose that there is $H$ feet of water behind the dam. Then the total force on the dam is given by

$$F(H) = \int_0^H p(H - h)w\,dh,$$

where $p = 62.5$ lb/ft$^3$ is the weight-density of water. Thus, $F(H)$ is the total force on the dam when there is $H$ feet of water behind it. Since the Interpolant nearly dries up in the late summer and rages in the spring, $H$

may vary from 0 to 100, the height of the dam, after which it would simply spill over the top.

BEAVER would like to have a graph of the function $F(H)$. You can certainly produce this by simply doing numerical integration for lots of values of $H$ (say 100) and plotting the results. Unfortunately, most of your computing resources budget at ACME has been used up for the fiscal year. This means that if you solve this problem in the straightforward way, you are going to have a computing cost overrun for the fiscal year which is going to come out of your salary. This puts you in a tight spot: either solve the problem and take a pay cut, or don't solve the problem and lose your job.

Luckily, you know enough about numerical methods to figure out a way to save both your job and your salary. It's a bit subtle, but it should work. After producing a graph of the function, turn in the graph, a listing of the FORTRAN program you used to estimate $F(H)$, and a written report describing what you did. Explain how much computer time (at least in terms of the number of integrals you had to evaluate) you think you saved by being clever. Bear in mind that federal reporting standards require the hydrostatic pressure of all dams on the Interpolant River to be given in tons. You may find the following hints helpful:

**Hint 1:** You should be able to get by with only ten calls to the NAG routine D01AJF. However, since you want to plot a smooth curve, you can fill in gaps by doing spline interpolation. The NAG routines E02BAF and E02BCF can be used for this purpose. In the call to E02BAF, let M=11. This means that NCAP7=15 in the routine E02BCF.

**Hint 2:** Evaluate the spline at lots of points. These evaluations are much cheaper than the evaluation of integrals, and they are rather accurate approximations to the integrals. Thus, it is easy to estimate the hydrostatic pressure at, say, 200 points by evaluating the spline.

**Hint 3:** Don't forget the federal reporting standards!

**Hint 4:** The routine E01BAF from the NAG FORTRAN Library is easier to use than E02BAF. Use it if it is available.

# Project 16

---

ACME is currently under contract to help the Corporation Of Nuclear Electrical Devices, one of the nation's largest commercial producers of electricity, build a laser fusion reactor. This reactor will be powered by a single strong laser pulse targeted at some small object in the middle of this device. The details of how this works are unimportant, but the characteristics of the laser pulse, at least for this particular project, are crucial.

The people in CON ED's laboratory have made several measurements of the laser pulse during the time when it is turned on, but they still have no idea what the pulse looks like as a function of time. Because of your excellent reputation in doing numerical computations, the people at CON ED have decided that they would like to have you produce a picture of this function. Your boss has agreed that you are just the person for the job.

The power produced by the pulse can be considered a function of time, say $P(t)$. The measurements produced by CON ED are the total energy of the pulse during the first second of operation, the first and second moments of the power function, and two pieces of spectral information. More precisely, CON ED has measured the following numbers which estimate the given integrals:

$$0.43843 = \int_0^1 P(t)dt$$

$$0.16475 = \int_0^1 tP(t)dt$$

$$0.07844 = \int_0^1 t^2 P(t)dt$$

$$0.33298 = \int_0^1 \sin(\pi t)P(t)dt$$

$$0.14434 = \int_0^1 \cos(\pi t)P(t)dt$$

You will approximate $P(t)$ by a function $S(t)$ which has the form

$$S(t) = a_1 + a_2 t + a_3 t^2 + a_4 \sin(\pi t) + a_5 \cos(\pi t).$$

Thus, it will be your job to compute the $a_i$. This is done by **projecting** $P(t)$ onto the space of functions which are of the same form as $S(t)$ above. That is, you insist that the five equations

$$\int_0^1 S(t)dt = \int_0^1 P(t)dt$$

$$\int_0^1 tS(t)dt = \int_0^1 tP(t)dt$$

$$\int_0^1 t^2S(t)dt = \int_0^1 t^2P(t)dt$$

$$\int_0^1 \sin(\pi t)S(t)dt = \int_0^1 \sin(\pi t)P(t)dt$$

$$\int_0^1 \cos(\pi t)S(t)dt = \int_0^1 \cos(\pi t)P(t)dt$$

be satisfied. Once you have computed the $a_i$, you have a function which should be a good approximation to $P(t)$. Produce a graph of this function in the interval $[0, 1]$.

Be sure to hand in an explanation of how you solved this problem and why you think your approximation is the best possible approximation given only the five measurements provided by CON ED. The following hint should help you to complete this project, which is vital in terms of providing future energy to the world:

**Hint 1:** You are going to have to use the NAG routine D01AJF 14 or 15 times. (You can avoid this by evaluating each of these integrals analytically, but that is not what we are in the business of doing). In addition, you are going to have to solve one $5 \times 5$ linear system of equations, using F01BTF and F04AYF. If you find that there are some non-linear equations appearing, you have gone astray.

# Project 17

The Dependable Industrial Reprehensible Toxic Yuck company, a national chemical company, is having trouble at one of its many plants. It seems that many of the employees are developing a strange disease. DIRTY claims that the disease is caused by a virus which just happens to be going around, but the Environmental Protection Agency isn't quite so sure, and it has hired the Corporate Liaison for Engineering Air Niceness, a division of ACME, to investigate the matter.

The plant in question produces a chemical called *convexitygen*, a chemical with many industrial uses (it is used in the manufacture of *cramerrulic*, for example). The reaction which produces *convexitygen* takes place in a fairly simple reactor. Two compounds, *arithmetic acid* and *boundary valuum* are placed in the reactor. They react to form *convexitygen*. However, the *convexitygen* reacts with the *boundary valuum* to produce a waste chemical, *determinantanol*, which is quite toxic. The *determinantanol* then decomposes into *arithmetic acid* and *boundary valuum*. If $a$, $b$, $c$, and $d$ represent, respectively, the concentrations of *arithmetic acid*, *boundary valuum*, *convexitygen*, and *determinantanol* present in the reactor, then the differential equations governing this reaction are:

$$
\begin{aligned}
a' &= \lambda_1 d - 0.5\lambda_3 ab \\
b' &= \lambda_2 d - 0.5\lambda_3 ab - 0.5\lambda_4 bc \\
c' &= \lambda_3 ab - 0.5\lambda_4 bc \\
d' &= \lambda_4 bc - (\lambda_1 + \lambda_2)d,
\end{aligned}
\tag{1}
$$

where $\lambda_1$, $\lambda_2$, $\lambda_3$, and $\lambda_4$ are constants depending upon the various catalysts which might be used in the reactor.

DIRTY is under suspicion because of the nature of this reaction. It turns out that whenever *determinantanol* is present in a greater concentration than *convexitygen*, trace amounts of it can leak out of the reactor, poisoning the atmosphere nearby. Workers who happen to inhale the gas become quite ill. The Environmental Protection Agency suspects that this is happening, but DIRTY will not allow an investigation team on the premises. Thus, CLEAN has been hired to figure out whether or not a court order to shut down DIRTY's facility is in order. Since on-sight measurements are out of the question, the equations (1) are going to have to be solved numerically to determine what it going on inside the reactor. Your boss at ACME has assigned you to the project.

One of DIRTY's employees, who was among the first to become seriously ill on the job and who happens to know the value of the $\lambda$'s in the reactor in question, has volunteered the information in the hope that the health of many of his fellow employees can be saved. Thus, it is known that $\lambda_1 = \lambda_2 = 0.2$, $\lambda_3 = 8.0$, and $\lambda_4 = 10.0$. In addition, the reactor is initially loaded with 50 per cent *arithmetic acid* and 50 per cent *boundary valuum*. Once the reaction starts, it is allowed to run for ten hours (the time scale for equations (1) is in hours), at which time it is shut down, the contents are drained, and the process is restarted. Your job is to determine whether or not the concentration of *determinantanol* exceeds the concentration of *convexitygen* at any time during this ten-hour period.

You will do this by writing a FORTRAN program to solve equations (1) by calling the NAG routine D02BBF. You should hand in to your boss a listing of your rather short, but nonetheless well-documented, program, an explanation of how you produced the results that you did, and your recommendation to the judge concerning the court order for DIRTY's plant.

# Project 18

ACME is conducting an important experiment aboard the space shuttle *Discovery* on its historic mission to the Asteroid Belt between Mars and Jupiter. Because of the importance of these experiments, you have been ordered to go along to assist. While you have been assigned several other important computations to perform during the six month flight, you have also been assigned the task of assisting the navigator during the mission.

In particular, it will be your job to help the navigator avoid the asteroids. There will be one part of the journey that will be especially tricky for the pilot to steer. Three rather large asteroids will be in the vicinity of *Discovery* within a particular ten-hour period of time. You are going to have to compute and plot the trajectories of these three asteroids during that ten-hour period.

Fortunately, the motion of these three things is planar, so that only a two-dimensional computation is necessary. At the start of this ten-hour period, and in appropriate coordinates, assuming that *Discovery* is at $(0, 0)$, *Approximant*, the largest of the asteroids with a mass of $3 \times 10^{19}$ kg, is at $(100\,000, 100\,000)$, i.e. $100\,000$ m away in each of two perpendicular directions. *Barycentric*, with a mass of $1 \times 10^{19}$ kg, is located at $(100\,000, 900\,000)$, and *Chebyshev*, with a mass of $2 \times 10^{19}$ kg is located at $(900\,000, 900\,000)$. Initially, *Barycentric* is moving straight towards *Approximant* with a speed of $100\,000$ m/hour, *Chebyshev* is moving straight towards *Barycentric* with a speed of $40\,000$ m / hour, and *Approximant* is travelling parallel to the line between *Barycentric* and *Chebyshev* towards *Chebyshev* with a speed of $150\,000$ m/hour.

Because everything is in the Sun's, as well as Jupiter's, gravitational field, these forces can be neglected. The mass of *Discovery* can also be neglected. In fact, everything except the gravitational force of the three asteroids can be neglected. Thus, if $x_1$, $x_2$, and $x_3$ represent the (vector) positions of *Approximant*, *Barycentric*, and *Chebyshev*, respectively, then the motion of the three asteroids is described by the classical $n$ body problem. This problem, which has been studied since the time of Newton, is given, for the case $n = 3$, by the following system of ordinary differential equations

$$m_1 x_1'' = f_{12}(x_2 - x_1)/r_{12} + f_{13}(x_3 - x_1)/r_{13}$$
$$m_2 x_2'' = f_{12}(x_1 - x_2)/r_{12} + f_{23}(x_3 - x_2)/r_{23}$$
$$m_3 x_3'' = f_{13}(x_1 - x_3)/r_{13} + f_{23}(x_2 - x_3)/r_{23}$$

Here, $m_1$, $m_2$, and $m_3$ represent the masses of the three asteroids, and $r_{ij}$ is the distance between $x_i$ and $x_j$ at time $t$. The three $f_{ij}$ are the gravitational forces acting on the asteroids. In particular,

$$f_{ij} = \frac{Gm_i m_j}{r_{ij}^2},$$

where $G$ is the universal gravitation constant. Because the time-scale for this problem is in hours (not seconds), this constant is

$$G = 8.6443 \times 10^{-4} \frac{\text{m}^3}{\text{hour}^2 \text{kg}}.$$

Your task for the navigator is to solve this system of equations and plot the three trajectories. You should use the NAG routine D02BBF to solve the differential equations. A tolerance of $10^{-4}$ is sufficient to obtain reasonable results. Solve the differential equation for a ten-hour period starting with the initial positions described above. Write a work report detailing what you had to do in order to solve the problem. You may find the following hints helpful:

**Hint 1:** When calling D02BBF, N=12.

**Hint 2:** The parameter T in your routine FCN (which need not have that name, but is nonetheless required by D02BBF), is never used.

# Project 19

The city of Cyborg has a problem. It has just been invaded by *malfunctionis equipmentatis*, a species of insect which likes to nest inside high-tech electrical equipment. Unfortunately, this peculiar nesting habit is wreaking havoc throughout Cyborg, since the bugs are causing equipment failures everywhere. In order to combat this infestation, the Cyborg city council has asked Quellers United Against Surviving Hexapods, a local exterminating company, to submit a bid for spraying to eliminate the pests. Simultaneously, it has hired the National Unit for Insecticide Spraying to Aid a Nice, Clean Environment, a division of ACME, to study the situation. Assuming that QUASH gets the contract to spray to eliminate the pests, it will be the job of NUISANCE to determine the effects of the spraying.

For some reason, you have been assigned to this project. Your briefing papers are deliberately vague, and it is not at all clear just how your presence is going to be helpful. However, ACME has flown you to Cyborg to join the team from NUISANCE, so you have taken your camera along to take pictures of butterflies and birds as it is very unlikely that there will be much else for you to do there. After stopping at a bookstore to buy a butterfly book, you decide to spend the day at the park.

Later in the day you notice a particularly colorful butterfly that you have never seen before. Thinking back on it, however, you realize that you have been seeing many of them all day. After consulting your book, you identify it as *erratus correctus*, a very rare species. After pondering for a few moments why there seem to be so many of them around, you forget all about it and decide to rejoin some of your NUISANCE acquaintances for dinner.

During dinner, however, you happen to mention to the NUISANCE insect specialist that you have been watching *erratus correctus* all day. He remarks that although the species is native to this part of the country, it is highly unusual to have seen it, since it is very rare indeed. This time, your curiousity is truly piqued, and you head for the local library as soon as dinner ends. It is here that you learn that the adult members of the species *erratus correctus* feed on the larvae of *malfunctionis equipmentatis*. No wonder you have seen so many of them! There is an overabundance of food for them to eat right in Cyborg.

Being the mathematical sort that you are, you decide that perhaps you can contribute to the NUISANCE study after all. After a little thought, you develop the following model of the situation:

$$e'(t) = -c_1 e(t) - \alpha e(t) + c_2 e(t)m(t) - c_3 e(t)^2$$
$$m'(t) = c_4 m(t) - \alpha m(t) - c_5 e(t)m(t) - c_6 m(t)^2,$$

where $e(t)$ is the number of *errati correcti* at time $t$ (in millions), $m(t)$ is the number of *malfunctionae equipmentatae* at $t$ (also in millions), $\alpha$ is the amount of spraying that is done, and the $c_i$ are constants which are particular to the two species. These equations model the iteration of the two insect populations in such a way that the effects of spraying can be predicted. You decide to attempt to determine the correct amount of spray that should be used ($\alpha$ is measured in liters/hectare).

What you have decided to do initially is to predict the insect populations for various values of $\alpha$ between 0 and 0.5 (higher amounts of spray will start to cause harm to the human population of the area). You intend to get a good idea of what is going on by doing this, after which you will formulate the appropriate minimization problem (minimize $m(7)$, the *malfunctionis equipmentatis* population 7 days from now, as a function of $\alpha$). One of the NUISANCE people has already obtained much of the information you need. She estimates the current population at 200 million, while her estimate of the local *erratus correctus* population is 4 million. Between the library, your butterfly book, and the NUISANCE insect specialist, you have been able to estimate the values of the $c_i$. For this problem, they turn out to be $c_1 = 0.435$, $c_2 = 0.002$, $c_3 = 0.02$, $c_4 = 6.098$, $c_5 = 0.3$, and $c_6 = 0.02$. With this information, you decide to solve your model for 50 to 100 different values of $\alpha$, just to get a feeling for what is going on.

Once you are done, you immediately rush off to see the NUISANCE project leader. He thinks your results are absurd. However, you persevere and win your chance to speak before the Cyborg city council. You decide to prepare a brief describing your findings, your results, and your explanation of those results. The last part will have to be particularly well-written, since it is unlikely that many people are going to believe you. Why? You may find the following hints helpful:

**Hint 1:** Use the NAG routine D02BBF to solve the differential equations.

**Hint 2:** In order to complete the project, it will be necessary for you to interpret your results. Thus, the written project report is of even more importance than usual. In order to convince others that you are not crazy, it will be necessary for you to correctly explain why your answers are what they are. You will not need to formulate or solve the minimization problem (although this would normally be a good idea). Explain why.

**Hint 3:** What you have observed (or should have observed) is called Volterra's phenomenon and is fairly well-studied. How could this problem be solved better using the NAG routine E04VDF?

**Postscript:** After all is said and done, you are sued by QUASH for damages to their livelihood. However, the ACME attorneys are able to convince them of the absurdity of their case, and they agree to drop the lawsuit if you agree to never again set foot in Cyborg. You are only too happy to comply.

# Project 20

The Telephone Operators Union for Calling Home is unhappy about the quality of the telephone lines in one of their main districts. As it turns out, a subsidiary of ACME, the Reprehensible Enterprise for Auditory Communication and Hearing, a local telephone company, is responsible for maintaining the phone lines in that district. In response to the complaints from TOUCH, REACH has ordered new fiber optic cables to install to replace the worn out copper wires still in service. Another division of ACME, the Organization for Using Telephones, manufactures optic fibers, and they will be supplying the new materials for REACH.

Optic fiber manufacture is a tricky business, though, and because REACH is determined to improve the quality of its phone lines, they are insisting on using high quality optic fibers. In order for OUT to be able to produce fibers of this quality, there is one engineering difficulty that is going to have to be ironed out. This involves a computation to determine just how fast the silicon rods should be fed into the furnace to produce the desired optic fibers. It will be your job to help the people at REACH, OUT, and TOUCH. Someone there has specifically asked for you, since by now you have an ACME-wide reputation for doing an excellent job.

Optic fibers are produced by taking a silicon rod, usually about one centimeter in diameter and feeding it through a hot furnace. This causes the rod to soften, and as it does, it gets pulled into a very fine fiber, usually just a fraction of a millimeter in diameter. At the end of the furnace is a take-up spool onto which the newly produced optical fiber is wound. The spool attempts to reel in the fiber a little bit too quickly, so the fiber itself is always under tension. This means that the rate at which the fiber is produced is determined by the diameter of the original rod, the ultimate thickness of the fiber, and the temperature of the furnace.

The OUT furnace is set to 2300 K, which is quite hot indeed. It is 25 centimeters long. The differential equations which describe the manufacture of optic fibers are:

$$s'(x) = -\frac{1}{u_0} f(t(x))s(x)$$
$$t'(x) = -\frac{C}{u_0} s(x)(t(x)^4 - t_f^4),$$

where $t_f$ is the temperature of the furnace and

$$f(t) = \left\{ \begin{array}{ll} Be^{A/(t_s-t)}, & t > t_s \\ 0, & t \le t_s. \end{array} \right\}$$

These equations describe the radius (in centimeters) of the optic fiber, $s$, and the temperature of the optic fiber, $t$, as functions of the position of the rod / fiber in the furnace. Here, $t_s$ is the critical temperature at which the silicon rod begins to soften. For the particular rods that OUT uses, $t_s = 1900$ K. The constants $A$, $B$, and $C$ depend upon the specific gravity of the silicon rods, the viscosity of soft rods, the elasticity of the materials, etc. For this particular application, OUT has set things up so that $A = 1$, $B = 0.1$, and $C = 10^{-11}$. The number $u_0$ describes the rate (in cm / sec) at which rods are fed into the furnace. Rods which have a diameter of 1.2 centimeters will be used. It is desired to produce fibers which have a radius of 0.1 millimeters. Thus, OUT needs to know how fast to feed rods in in order to achieve this. In other words, they need to know the correct value of $u_0$.

You are going to have to solve for this number. You should assume that the rods are initially at room temperature (293.16 K). Write a FORTRAN program which does this. Your program should produce a graph of the radius function as output. Thus, you should see a profile of the rod as it travels through the furnace. In order to satisfy your boss, produce a well-written project report describing what you had to do in order to solve this problem. Hand in a listing of your program, your final graph, the computed rate at which rods should be fed into the furnace, and your report describing what you did. You may find the following hints helpful.

**Hint 1:** The NAG routine D02HBF should be used. It will do most of the work for you.

**Hint 2:** In D02HBF, let N=2 and N1=1.

**Hint 3:** The first two hints are not really hints. They are project requirements. Do not try to find an alternative way of solving the problem.

# Project 21

---

The Big Remote Army Supply Station, a military installation of great importance to the defense of much of the western world, has just been penetrated by an agent working for the Spaceage Proliferation of Industrial Espionage Society. The security people working at BRASS have discovered that the agent, working from the inside, managed to secure blueprints for an important new jet.

Fortunately, the SPIES agent has not yet had an opportunity to deliver the plans, so there is still a chance of capturing him before he reports his findings. By working with BRASS, American Intelligence has learned that the agent is currently hiding in a small boat moored some distance offshore. Blackford Oakes, the man that American Intelligence has sent to recapture the agent, is quite capable and daring, and he intends to seize the boat by parachuting onto it under cover of darkness. It is necessary to capture the agent alive, for BRASS needs to be sure that SPIES has caused no other breeches of security.

In order to maintain surprise, BRASS has suggested the use of a Hyped Up Silent Helicopter, which is manufactured by United Planes, a division of ACME. Because the HUSH is still experimental, UP has the only pilots trained to fly it. For security reasons, BRASS is insisting that a minimal crew consisting of Blackford Oakes, who will do the actual parachuting, a pilot, and one other person, responsible for selecting the jump point, be assembled. Your boss at ACME has chosen you for this delicate assignment, since you have demonstrated time and again your ability for performing accurate, useful computations.

The plan of attack is as follows. The boat upon which Blackford Oakes will attempt to land is located at a certain point. The pilot is going to fly the HUSH directly over the boat (because it is dark and the helicopter is silent, both to the ear and to radar, the chances of being detected are slim). The HUSH is to be flown at a constant altitude of 1000 meters and a constant horizontal speed of 50 meters / second. At a position selected by you, Blackford Oakes is going to jump out of the plane and open his chute immediately. He will then float down to the boat, capture the agent, and return the boat to port.

The differential equations describing this situation are given by:

$$x''(t) = [W(y) - x'(t)]\psi$$
$$y''(t) = -g - y'(t)\psi,$$

(1)

where $g$, the acceleration due to gravity, is 9.8 m sec$^{-2}$,

$$\psi = \alpha\sqrt{[W(y) - x'(t)]^2 + [y'(t)]^2},$$

and $W(y)$ is the velocity of the wind at altitude $y$. Here, $\alpha$ is a parameter which is determined by the size and aerodynamic characteristics of the parachute. Blackford Oakes' chute has $\alpha = 0.6$.

Unfortunately, $W(y)$ is an unknown function, so you are going to have to approximate it. The HUSH is equipped with a wind gauge capable of measuring the velocity of the wind at 100-meter intervals all the way to the ground. In addition, the pilot plans to choose a direction so that there is no crosswind. The measurements from the wind gauge will then be used to construct a cubic spline approximation to $W(y)$.

If you assume that the boat is located at the point $x = 0, y = 0$, (and you will assume this), then the HUSH is located along the line $y = 1000$. You must determine the following things in order to determine when Blackford Oakes is going to jump out of the plane: the position along the line $y = 1000$ where the jump should occur, the impact velocity of Oakes when he hits the boat, and the amount of time it takes for him to reach the ground. All of these things may be computed simultaneously using the NAG routine D02HBF.

The wind during the time of the flyover has been measured and is displayed in the table below:

| ALTITUDE | WIND (m/sec) |
|---|---|
| 1000 | 3.6 |
| 900 | 2.3 |
| 800 | 1.2 |
| 700 | −1.8 |
| 600 | −6.8 |
| 500 | −17.6 |
| 400 | −19.3 |
| 300 | −12.2 |
| 200 | −10.2 |
| 100 | −9.2 |
| 0 | −8.8 |

The cubic spline approximation to the function $W(y)$ should be constructed using the NAG routine E02BAF and evaluated using E02BCF.

As usual, you should turn in a report detailing what you have done. It should include, among other things, the initial jump point, the final velocity, a computer-generated graph of the trajectory, and time it takes to reach the ground. It should also explain any other oddities that might occur. You may find the following hints helpful.

**Hint 1:** When calling D02HBF, N=4 and N1=2. In addition, when calling E02BCF, the value of NCAP7 should be 15.

**Hint 2:** You will need to use a common block in order to pass the cubic spline information to where it is required.

**Hint 3:** Get started early. These three NAG routines are rather sensitive. It may take a bit of fiddling around in order to get them to do what you want.

**Hint 4:** If the routine E01BAF is available, it may be substituted for E02BAF. E01BAF is easier to use and accomplishes the same thing.

# Project 22

The Modern Electronic Lifting Team, a division of ACME, is designing a grabber arm for the Humble Automatic Lackey 9000, ACME's industrial robot (mentioned in Project 1 and Project 12). The grabber arm is intended to enable HAL to grab objects which are much too hot for him to grab directly. Because the competition from the AJAX Newfangled Electronic Robotic Device (mentioned in Project 12) is so stiff, MELT needs to minimize its costs as much as possible when designing and building the grabber arm. MELT has asked SOLVE for assistance with this design problem, and Biro Kratt has decided that the problem is important enough to warrant putting his best person on the project, so you have been asked to help out.

The main component of the grabber arm is a metal dowel made up of a mixture of two alloys, namely *insulatinum* and *conductivitum*. One end of the dowel will be exposed to temperatures as high as 850 K, while the other end will be attached directly to HAL, who cannot tolerate temperatures in excess of 375 K without suffering thermal circuitry failure. You have been asked to design the MELT dowel so that HAL does not fail.

The temperature distribution of the dowel must satisfy the heat equation:

$$\kappa(x)u''(x) + \kappa'(x)u'(x) = 0,$$

where $u$ is the temperature of the dowel at position $x$, and $\kappa(x)$ is the thermal conductivity of the dowel, which depends upon its composition. In this case, the temperature distribution should satisfy the boundary conditions

$$u(0) = 850$$
$$u'(L) + 0.01u(L) = 0,$$

where $L$ is the length of the dowel. The first boundary condition states that the temperature on one end is 850 K. The second boundary condition is the radiation boundary condition, which states that HAL will absorb thermal energy from the rod. The thermal conductivity depends upon the relative density of *insulatinum* in the rod, and it is given by

$$\kappa(x) = 4\rho(x)^2 - 5\rho(x) + 2,$$

where $\rho(x)$ is the relative density of *insulatinum* in the rod. MELT knows that the cost of the two alloys are such that a one centimeter dowel of pure *insulatinum* costs \$80, while a one centimeter dowel of pure *conductivitum* costs \$30. Thus, the total cost of the dowel is given by

$$c = \int_0^L [8\rho(x) + 3(1 - \rho(x))]dx.$$

Your job is to determine the function $\rho$ and the length of the dowel $L$ such that the total cost of the rod is minimized, subject to the constraint that $u(L) \leq 375$, which prevents HAL from overheating. You should find the following hints helpful:

**Hint 1:** You can model $\rho$ with a cubic spline. Divide the interval $[0, L]$ into some number of pieces (say 8), and let $\rho$ be completely determined by the coefficients of the spline. This discretizes the problem by replacing the problem of determining a function to one of determining a fixed number of coefficients. You will find the NAG routines E02BCF and E02BDF very helpful in this context.

**Hint 2:** The NAG routine E04VDF can be used to minimize the cost. When you call this routine, it should have one non-linear constraint, which should say something about preventing HAL from overheating. The remainder of the constraints should be simple constraints on the spline coefficients which model $\rho$. Since the value of a spline is bounded by its coefficients, forcing $0 \leq \rho(x) \leq 1$ for all $x$ amounts to imposing the same condition on each of the coefficients.

**Hint 3:** You need to provide derivatives to E04VDF for the objective function and for the non-linear constraint. The derivatives for the objective function are easy, since the objective function depends linearly on the spline coefficients. Thus, you can compute the derivative with respect to each of the spline coefficients by calling E02BDF. The remaining derivative (the one with respect to $L$) can be determined by the fundamental theorem of calculus. The derivatives of the non-linear constraint are a little harder. You can determine an appropriate initial value problem for the derivatives with respect to the spline coefficients which can be solved, but this yields a pretty big mess. What is conceptually easier, and perhaps computationally less intense, is to compute these derivatives using divided differences. Thus, to get the derivative with respect to one of the coefficients, say $c_i$, compute $u(L)$ using $c_i$ and again using $c_i + \varepsilon$, for some small value of $\varepsilon$. Then

$$\frac{\partial}{\partial c_i} u(L) \approx \frac{u(L; c_i + \varepsilon) - u(L; c_i)}{\varepsilon}.$$

This can be computed for each $i$. The derivative of $u(L)$ with respect to $L$ is given by $-0.01u(L)$. Why?

# Documentation

---

The following pages contain excerpts from the NAG FORTRAN Workstation Library documentation. More complete documentation may be found in the NAG FORTRAN Workstation Library Manuals. Before using any of these routines, please refer to the appropriate Appendix of the NAG FORTRAN Workstation Library Manuals to determine the interpretation of **bold italicized** terms and other implementation dependent details. In particular, the routine name may be precision dependent. Thus, in certain implementations, the last letter of the routine name may be different, and **real** may be interpreted as DOUBLE PRECISION.

The pages that follow have been reprinted by permission of NAG, Ltd. The copyright of the following pages remains the property of NAG, Ltd.

# C05ADF

## 1. Purpose

C05ADF locates a zero of a continuous function in a given interval by a combination of the methods of linear interpolation, extrapolation and bisection.

## 2. Specification

```
      SUBROUTINE C05ADF (A, B, EPS, ETA, F, X, IFAIL)
C     INTEGER    IFAIL
C     real       A, B, EPS, ETA, F, X
C     EXTERNAL   F
```

## 3. Description

The routine attempts to obtain an approximation to a simple zero of the function $f(x)$ given an initial interval $[a,b]$ such that $f(a) \times f(b) \leq 0$.

The approximation x to the zero $\alpha$ is determined so that one or both of the following criteria are satisfied:

(i)  $|x - \alpha| <$ EPS,

(ii)  $|f(x)| <$ ETA.

## 4. References

None.

## 5. Parameters

A – *real*.

On entry, A must specify a, the lower bound of the interval.

Unchanged on exit.

B – *real*.

On entry, B must specify b, the upper bound of the interval.

Unchanged on exit.

EPS – *real*.

On entry, EPS must specify the absolute tolerance to which the zero is required (see Section 3).

EPS $> 0.0$.

Unchanged on exit.

ETA – *real*.

On entry, ETA must specify a value such that if $|f(x)| <$ ETA, x is accepted as the zero $\alpha$. ETA may be specified as 0.0 (see Section 7).

Unchanged on exit.

F – *real* FUNCTION, supplied by the user.

F defines the function f whose zero is to be determined.

Its specification is:

*real* FUNCTION    F(XX)
*real*             XX

XX – *real*.

On entry, XX specifies the point at which the value of the function is to be evaluated. XX must not be changed in the function F.

F must be declared as EXTERNAL in the (sub)program from which C05ADF is called.

X – *real*.

On exit, X contains the approximation to the zero $\alpha$ of the function f(x).

IFAIL – INTEGER.

Before entry, IFAIL must be set to 0 or 1. For users not familiar with this parameter (described in the Introduction to this Handbook) the recommended value is 0.

Unless the routine detects an error (see next section), IFAIL contains 0 on exit.

## 6. Error Indicators and Warnings

Errors detected by the routine:

IFAIL = 1

On entry,  EPS $\leq$ 0,
or         A = B,
or         F(A)$\times$F(B)>0.

IFAIL = 2

Too much accuracy has been requested in the computation, that is, EPS is too small for the computer being used. The final value of X is an accurate approximation to the zero $\alpha$.

IFAIL = 3

A change in sign of f(x) has been determined as occurring near the point defined by the final value of X. However, there is some evidence that this sign-change corresponds to a pole of f(x).

IFAIL = 4

Indicates that a serious error has occurred in auxiliary routine C05AZF.

Check all routine calls. Seek expert help.

## 7. Accuracy

This depends on the value of EPS and ETA. If full machine accuracy is required, they may be set very small, resulting in an error exit with IFAIL = 2, although this may involve many more iterations than a lesser accuracy. The user is recommended to set ETA = 0.0 and to use EPS to control the accuracy, unless he has considerable knowledge of the size of f(x) for values x near the zero $\alpha$.

## 8. Further Comments

Timing depends primarily on the time spent evaluating F (see Section 5).

# D01AJF

## 1. Purpose

D01AJF is a general-purpose integrator which calculates an approximation to the integral of a function F(x) over a finite interval [A,B]:

$$I = \int_{A}^{B} F(x)\, dx.$$

## 2. Specification

```
      SUBROUTINE D01AJF (F, A, B, EPSABS, EPSREL, RESULT, ABSERR,
     1                   W, LW, IW, LIW, IFAIL)
C     INTEGER      LW, IW(LIW), LIW, IFAIL
C     real         F, A, B, EPSABS, EPSREL, RESULT, ABSERR, W(LW)
C     EXTERNAL     F
```

## 3. Description

D01AJF is based upon the QUADPACK [3] routine DQAGS. It is an adaptive routine, using the Gauss 10-point and Kronrod 21-point rules. The algorithm, described in [1], incorporates a global acceptance criterion (as defined by Malcolm and Simpson [2]) together with the $\varepsilon$-algorithm [4] to perform extrapolation. The local error estimation is described in [3].

The routine is suitable as a general-purpose integrator, and can be used when the integrand has singularities, especially when these are of algebraic or logarithmic type.

## 4. References

[1]  DE DONCKER, E.
     An adaptive extrapolation algorithm for automatic integration.
     Signum Newsletter 13, No. 2, pp. 12-18, 1978.

[2]  MALCOLM, M.A. and SIMPSON, R.B.
     Local versus global strategies for adaptive quadrature.
     A.C.M. Trans. Math. Software 1, pp. 129-146, 1976.

[3]  PIESSENS, R., DE DONCKER, E., ÜBERHUBER, C. and KAHANER, D.
     'QUADPACK', A Subroutine Package for Automatic Integration.
     Springer-Verlag, 1983.

[4]  WYNN, P.
     On a device for computing the $e_m$ $(S_n)$ transformation.
     Math. Tables Aids Comp., 10, pp. 91-96, 1956.

## 5. Parameters

F – *real* FUNCTION, supplied by the user.

F must return the value of the integrand at a given point.

Its specification is:

```
real FUNCTION    F(X)
real             X
```

X – *real*.

On entry, X specifies the point at which the integrand value is required by D01AJF.

X must not be reset by F.

F must be declared as EXTERNAL in the (sub)program from which D01AJF is called.

A – *real*.

On entry, A must specify the lower limit of integration.

Unchanged on exit.

B – *real*.

On entry, B must specify the upper limit of integration.

Unchanged on exit.

EPSABS – *real*.

On entry, EPSABS must specify the absolute accuracy required. If EPSABS is negative, the absolute value is used. See Section 7.

Unchanged on exit.

EPSREL – *real*.

On entry, EPSREL must specify the relative accuracy required. If EPSREL is negative, the absolute value is used. See Section 7.

Unchanged on exit.

RESULT – *real*.

On exit, RESULT contains the approximation to the integral I.

ABSERR – *real*.

On exit, ABSERR contains an estimate of the modulus of the absolute error, which should be an upper bound for $|I-RESULT|$.

W – *real* array of DIMENSION (LW).

Used as workspace.

LW – INTEGER.

On entry, LW must specify the dimension of W as declared in the (sub)program from which D01AJF is called. LW/4 is an upper bound for the number of subintervals into which the interval of integration is divided. A value in the range 800 to 2000 is adequate for. most problems. The more difficult the integrand, the larger LW should be. Trivially LW $\geq$ 4. See IW below.

LW is unchanged on exit.

IW – INTEGER array of DIMENSION (LIW).

Used as workspace.

On exit, IW(1) contains the amount of *real* workspace actually used (the smallest possible value of LW).

LIW – INTEGER.

On entry, LIW must specify the dimension of IW, as declared in the (sub)program from which D01AJF is called.

LIW $\geq$ LW/8 + 2.

Unchanged on exit.

IFAIL – INTEGER.

Before entry, IFAIL must be assigned a value. For users unfamiliar with this parameter (described in the Introduction to this Handbook) the recommended value is 0. Unless the routine detects an error (see next section), IFAIL contains 0 on exit.

**For this routine**, because the values of the output parameters may be useful even if IFAIL $\neq$ 0 on exit, users are recommended to set IFAIL to 1 before entry. **It is then essential to test the value of IFAIL on exit.**

## 6. Error Indicators and Warnings

Errors detected by the routine:

IFAIL = 1

The maximum number of subdivisions allowed with the given workspace has been reached without the accuracy requirements being achieved. Look at the integrand in order to determine the integration difficulties. If the position of a local difficulty within the interval can be determined (e.g. a singularity of the integrand or its derivative, a peak, a discontinuity...) one will probably gain from splitting up the interval at this point and calling the integrator on the subranges. If necessary, another integrator, which is designed for handling the type of difficulty involved, must be used. Alternatively consider relaxing the accuracy requirements specified by EPSABS and EPSREL, or increasing the amount of workspace.

IFAIL = 2

Roundoff error prevents the requested tolerance from being achieved. The error may be under-estimated. Consider requesting less accuracy.

IFAIL = 3

Extremely bad local integrand behaviour causes a very strong subdivision around one (or more) points of the interval. The same advice applies as in the case of IFAIL = 1.

IFAIL = 4

The requested tolerance cannot be achieved, because the extrapolation does not increase the accuracy satisfactorily: the returned result is the best which can be obtained. The same advice applies as in the case of IFAIL = 1.

IFAIL = 5

The integral is probably divergent, or slowly convergent. It must be noted that divergence can also occur with any non-zero value of IFAIL.

IFAIL = 6

On entry,  LW < 4,
or        LIW < LW/8 + 2.

## 7. Accuracy

The routine cannot guarantee, but in practice usually achieves, the following accuracy:

$$|I - \text{RESULT}| \leq \text{tol}$$

where

$$\text{tol} = \max\{|\text{EPSABS}|, |\text{EPSREL}| \times |I|\}.$$

Moreover it returns the quantity ABSERR which, in normal circumstances, satisfies

$$|I - \text{RESULT}| \leq \text{ABSERR} \leq \text{tol}.$$

## 8. Further Comments

Timing depends on the integrand and the accuracy required.

Labelled COMMON block AD01AJ is used by this routine and must therefore be avoided by the user.

# D02BBF

## 1. Purpose

D02BBF integrates a system of first-order ordinary differential equations over a range with suitable initial conditions, using a Runge-Kutta-Merson method, and returns the solution at points specified by the user.

## 2. Specification

```
      SUBROUTINE D02BBF (X, XEND, N, Y, TOL, IRELAB, FCN, OUTPUT,
     1                   W, IFAIL)
C     INTEGER    N, IRELAB, IFAIL
C     real       X, XEND, Y(N), TOL, W(N,7)
C     EXTERNAL   FCN, OUTPUT
```

## 3. Description

The routine integrates a system of ordinary differential equations

$$Y_i' = F_i(T,Y_1,Y_2,...,Y_N), \quad i = 1,2,...,N,$$

from $T = X$ to $T = XEND$ using a Merson form of the Runge-Kutta method. The system is defined by a subroutine FCN supplied by the user, which evaluates $F_i$ in terms of T and $Y_1,Y_2,...,Y_N$ (see Section 5), and the values of $Y_1,Y_2,...,Y_N$ given at $T = X$.

The solution is returned via the user-supplied routine OUTPUT at a set of points specified by the user. This solution is obtained by quintic Hermite interpolation on solution values produced by the Runge-Kutta method.

The accuracy of the integration and, indirectly, the interpolation is controlled by the parameters TOL and IRELAB.

For a description of Runge-Kutta methods and their practical implementation see [1].

## 4. References

[1] HALL, G. and WATT, J.M. (eds.)
Modern Numerical Methods for Ordinary Differential Equations.
Clarendon Press, Oxford, p. 59, 1976.

## 5. Parameters

X – *real*.

Before entry, X must be set to the initial value of the independent variable T.

On exit, it contains XEND, unless an error has occurred, when it contains the value of T at the error.

**XEND – *real*.**

On entry, XEND must specify the final value of the independent variable. If XEND < X on entry, integration will proceed in a negative direction.

Unchanged on exit.

**N – INTEGER.**

On entry, N must specify the number of differential equations.

Unchanged on exit.

**Y – *real* array of DIMENSION at least (N).**

Before entry, $Y(1),Y(2),...,Y(N)$ must contain the initial values of the solution $Y_1,Y_2,...,Y_N$.

On exit, $Y(1),Y(2),...,Y(N)$ contain the computed values of the solution at the final value of T.

**TOL – *real*.**

Before entry, TOL must be set to a **positive** tolerance for controlling the error in the integration. The routine D02BBF has been designed so that, for most problems, a reduction in TOL leads to an approximately proportional reduction in the error in the solution at XEND. The relation between changes in TOL and the error at intermediate output points is less clear, but for TOL small enough the error at intermediate output points should also be approximately proportional to TOL. However, the actual relation between TOL and the accuracy achieved cannot be guaranteed. The user is strongly recommended to call D02BBF with more than one value for TOL and to compare the results obtained to estimate their accuracy. In the absence of any prior knowledge, the user might compare the results obtained by calling D02BBF with $TOL = 10.0^{-P}$ and $TOL = 10.0^{-P-1}$ when P correct decimal digits are required in the solution.

TOL is normally unchanged on exit. However if the range X to XEND is so short that a small change in TOL is unlikely to make any change in the computed solution then, on return, TOL has its sign changed. This should be treated as a warning that the computed solution is likely to be more accurate than would be produced by using the same value of TOL on a longer range of integration.

**IRELAB – INTEGER.**

On entry, IRELAB determines the type of error control. At each step in the numerical solution an estimate of the local error, EST, is made. For the current step to be accepted the following condition must be satisfied:

IRELAB = 0

$EST \leq TOL \times \max\{1.0,|Y(1)|,|Y(2)|,...,|Y(N)|\};$

IRELAB = 1
   EST ≤ TOL;

IRELAB = 2
   EST ≤ TOL×max{eps,|Y(1)|,|Y(2)|,...,|Y(N)|},

where eps is given by X02AAF. If the appropriate condition is not satisfied, the stepsize is reduced and the solution is recomputed on the current step.

If the user wishes to measure the error in the computed solution in terms of the number of correct decimal places, then IRELAB should be given the value 1 on entry, whereas if the error requirement is in terms of the number of correct significant digits, then IRELAB should be given the value 2. Where there is no preference in the choice of error test IRELAB = 0 will result in a mixed error test.

Unchanged on exit.

FCN – SUBROUTINE, supplied by the user.

FCN must evaluate the functions $F_i$ (i.e. the derivatives $Y_i'$) for given values of its arguments $T,Y_1,...,Y_N$.

Its specification is:

```
SUBROUTINE FCN(T, Y, F)
real      T, Y(n), F(n)
```

where n is the actual value of N in the call of D02BBF.

T – *real*.

   On entry, T specifies the value of the argument T.

   Its value must not be changed.

Y – *real* array of DIMENSION (n).

   On entry, Y(I) contains the value of the argument $Y_I$, for I = 1,...,n.

   These values must not be changed.

F – *real* array of DIMENSION (n).

   On exit, F(I) must contain the value of $F_I$, for I = 1,...,n.

FCN must be declared as EXTERNAL in the (sub)program from which D02BBF is called.

OUTPUT – SUBROUTINE, supplied by the user.

   OUTPUT allows the user to have access to intermediate values of the computed solution (e.g. to print or plot them), at successive points specified by the user. It is initially called by D02BBF with XSOL = X (the initial value of T). The user must reset XSOL to the next point where OUTPUT is to be called, and so on at each call to OUTPUT. If, after a call to OUTPUT, the reset point XSOL is beyond XEND, D02BBF will integrate to XEND with no further calls to OUTPUT; if a call to OUTPUT is required at the point XSOL = XEND, then XSOL must be given precisely the value XEND.

Its specification is:

```
SUBROUTINE OUTPUT(XSOL, Y)
real        XSOL, Y(n)
```

where n is the actual value of N in the call of D02BBF.

### XSOL – *real*.

On entry, XSOL contains the current value of the independent variable T.

On exit, XSOL must contain the next value of T at which OUTPUT is to be called.

### Y – *real* array of DIMENSION (n).

On entry, Y contains the computed solution at the point XSOL.

Its elements must not be changed.

OUTPUT must be declared as EXTERNAL in the (sub)program from which D02BBF is called.

### W – *real* array of DIMENSION (N,p), where $p \geq 7$.

Used as working space.

### IFAIL – INTEGER.

Before entry, IFAIL must be set to 0 or 1. For users not familiar with this parameter (described in the Introduction to this Handbook) the recommended value is 0.

Unless the routine detects an error (see next section), IFAIL contains 0 on exit.

## 6. Error Indicators and Warnings

Errors detected by the routine:–

IFAIL = 1

On entry, $TOL \leq 0$
or $\qquad N \leq 0$
or $\qquad IRELAB \neq 0$, 1 or 2.

IFAIL = 2

With the given value of TOL, no further progress can be made across the integration range from the current point T = X, or the dependence of the error on TOL would be lost if further progress across the integration range were attempted (see Section 8 for a discussion of this error exit). The components Y(1),Y(2),...,Y(N) contain the computed values of the solution at the current point.

IFAIL = 3

TOL is too small for the routine to take an initial step (see Section 8). X and Y(1),Y(2),...,Y(N) retain their initial values.

IFAIL = 4

X = XEND and XSOL ≠ X after the initial call to OUTPUT.

IFAIL = 5

A value of XSOL returned by OUTPUT lies outside the current range X to XEND and lies closer to X than XEND.

IFAIL = 6

A serious error has occurred in an internal call to the auxiliary routine D02PAF. Check all subroutine calls and array dimensions. Seek expert help.

IFAIL = 7

A serious error has occurred in an internal call to the auxiliary routine D02XAF. Check all subroutine calls and array dimensions. Seek expert help.

## 7. Accuracy

The accuracy depends on TOL, on the mathematical properties of the differential system, on the length of the range of integration and on the method. It can be controlled by varying TOL but the approximate proportionality of the error to TOL holds only for a restricted range of values of TOL. For TOL too large, the underlying theory may break down and the result of varying TOL may be unpredictable. For TOL too small, rounding errors may affect the solution significantly and an error exit with IFAIL = 2 or IFAIL = 3 is possible.

At the intermediate output points the same remarks apply. For large values of TOL it is possible that the errors at some intermediate output points may be much larger than at XEND. In any case, it must not be expected that the error will have the same size at all output points. At any point, it is a combination of the errors arising from the integration of the differential equation and the interpolation. The effect of combining these errors will vary, though in most cases the integration error will dominate.

### 8. Further Comments

Timing depends on the complexity and mathematical properties of the system of differential equations defined by FCN, on the range, the tolerance and the number of calls to OUTPUT. There is also an overhead of the form $A + B \times N$ where A and B are machine-dependent computing times.

If the routine fails with IFAIL = 3, then it can be called again with a larger value of TOL if this has not already been tried. If the accuracy requested is really needed and cannot be obtained with this routine, the system may be very stiff (see below) or so badly scaled that it cannot be solved to the required accuracy.

If the routine fails with IFAIL = 2, it is probable that it has been called with a value of TOL which is so small that the solution cannot be obtained on the range X to XEND. This can happen for well-behaved systems and very small values of TOL. The user should, however, consider whether there is a more fundamental difficulty. For example:

in the region of a singularity (infinite value) of the solution, the routine will usually stop with IFAIL = 2, unless overflow occurs first. Numerical integration cannot be continued through a singularity, and analytic treatment should be considered;

for 'stiff' equations where the solution contains rapidly decaying components, the routine will use very small steps in T (internally to D02BBF) to preserve stability. This will exhibit itself by making the computing time excessively long, or occasionally by an exit with IFAIL = 2. Merson's method is not efficient in such cases, and the user should try the Gear method D02EBF.

For well-behaved systems with no difficulties such as stiffness or singularities, the Merson method should work well for low accuracy calculations (three or four figures). For high accuracy calculations or where FCN is costly to evaluate, Merson's method may not be appropriate and a computationally less expensive method may be the Adams method D02CBF.

# D02HBF

## 1. Purpose

D02HBF solves the two-point boundary-value problem for a system of ordinary differential equations, using initial value techniques and Newton iteration; it generalizes subroutine D02HAF to include the case where parameters other than boundary values are to be determined.

## 2. Specification

```
      SUBROUTINE D02HBF (P, N1, PE, E, N, SOLN, M1, FCN, BC, RANGE,
     1                   W, IW, IFAIL)
C     INTEGER     N1, N, M1, IW, IFAIL
C     real        P(N1), PE(N1), E(N), SOLN(N,M1), W(N,IW)
C     EXTERNAL    FCN, BC, RANGE
```

## 3. Description

The routine D02HBF solves the two-point boundary-value problem by determining the unknown parameters $P(1),P(2),...,P(N1)$ of the problem. These parameters may be, but need not be, boundary values; they may include eigenvalue parameters in the coefficients of the differential equations, length of the range of integration, etc. The notation and methods used are similar to those of D02HAF and the user is advised to study this first. (The parameters $P(1),P(2),...,P(N1)$ correspond precisely to the unknown boundary conditions in D02HAF.) It is assumed that we have a system of N first-order ordinary differential equations of the form:

$$\frac{dy_i}{dx} = f_i(x,y_1,y_2,...,y_N), \qquad i = 1,2,...,N,$$

and that the derivatives $f_i$ are evaluated by a subroutine FCN supplied by the user. The system, including the boundary conditions given by BC and the range of integration given by RANGE, involves the N1 unknown parameters $P(1),P(2),...,P(N1)$ which are to be determined, and for which initial estimates must be supplied. The number of unknown parameters N1 must not exceed the number of equations N. If $N1 < N$, we assume that $(N-N1)$ equations of the system are not involved in the matching process. These are usually referred to as 'driving equations'; they are independent of the parameters and of the solutions of the other N1 equations. In numbering the equations for the subroutine FCN, the driving equations must be put **first**.

The estimated values of the parameters are corrected by a form of Newton iteration. The Newton correction on each iteration is calculated using a Jacobian matrix whose (i,j)(th) element depends on the derivative of the i(th) component of the solution, $y_i$, with respect to the j(th) parameter, P(J). This matrix is calculated by a simple numerical differentiation technique which requires N1 integrations of the differential system.

If the parameter IFAIL is set appropriately, the routine automatically prints messages to inform the user of the flow of the calculation. These messages are discussed in detail in Section 8.

Routine D02HBF is a simplified version of routine D02SAF which is described in detail in [1].

## 4. References

[1] GLADWELL, I.
The Development of the Boundary Value Codes in the Ordinary Differential Equations Chapter of the NAG Library.
In: Codes for Boundary Value Problems in Ordinary Differential Equations,
Eds. Childs B., Scott M., Daniel J.W., Denman, E. and Nelson P.
Springer-Verlag Lecture Notes in Computer Science, Vol. 76, 1979.

## 5. Parameters

Users are strongly recommended to read Sections 3 and 8 in conjunction with this Section.

P – *real* array of DIMENSION (N1).

Before entry, P(I) must be set to an estimate for the I(th) parameter, for I = 1,2,...,N1.

On exit, it contains the corrected value for the I(th) parameter, unless an error has occurred, when it contains the last calculated value of the parameter.

N1 – INTEGER.

On entry, N1 must specify the number of parameters.

Unchanged on exit.

PE – *real* array of DIMENSION (N1).

Before entry, the elements of PE must be given positive values. The element PE(I) is used

(i) in the convergence test on the I(th) parameter in the Newton iteration, and

(ii)   in perturbing the I(th) parameter when approximating the derivatives of the components of the solution with respect to this parameter for use in the Newton iteration.

The elements PE(I) should not be chosen too small. They should usually be several orders of magnitude larger than EPS (the smallest *real* quantity such that $1.0 + EPS > 1.0$; see NAG Workstation Library routine X02AAF).

Unchanged on exit.

E – *real* array of DIMENSION (N).

Before entry, the elements of E must be given positive values. The element E(I) is used in the bound on the local error in the I(th) component of the solution $y_I$ during integration.

The elements E(I) should not be chosen too small. They should usually be several orders of magnitude larger than EPS (the smallest *real* quantity such that $1.0 + EPS > 1.0$).

Unchanged on exit.

N – INTEGER.

On entry, N must specify the total number of differential equations.

Unchanged on exit.

SOLN – *real* array of DIMENSION (N,M1).

On exit, SOLN contains the solution when $M1 > 1$ (see below). If $M1 = 1$ then the name of any array with at least N elements may be substituted for SOLN.

M1 – INTEGER.

On entry, M1 must specify a value which controls exit values as follows:

$M1 = 1$

The final solution is not calculated;

$M1 > 1$

The final values of the solution at interval (length of range)/$(M1-1)$ are calculated and stored sequentially in the array SOLN starting with the values of the solutions evaluated at the first end-point (see subroutine RANGE below) stored in the first column of SOLN.

Unchanged on exit.

FCN – SUBROUTINE, supplied by the user.

FCN must evaluate the function $f_i$ (i.e. the derivative $y'_i$), for i $=$ 1,2,...,N and place them in F(i).

Its specification is:

```
SUBROUTINE FCN(X, Y, F, P)
real       X, Y(n), F(n), P(n1)
```

where n and n1 are the actual values of N and N1 in the call of D02HBF.

X – *real*.

On entry, X specifies the value of the argument X.

Its value must not be changed.

Y – *real* array of DIMENSION (n).

On entry, Y(i) contains the value of the argument, $y_i$, for i $=$ 1,2,...,n.

These values must not be changed.

F – *real* array of DIMENSION (n).

On exit, F(i) must contain the derivative of $y_i$ evaluated at the point X, for i $=$ 1,2,...,n. F(i) may depend upon the parameters P(j), j $=$ 1,2,...,n1. If there are any driving equations (see Section 3) then these must be numbered first in the ordering of the components of F in FCN.

P – *real* array of DIMENSION (n1).

On entry, P(i) contains the current estimate of the i(th) parameter, for i $=$ 1,2,...,n1.

These values must not be changed.

FCN must be declared as EXTERNAL in the (sub)program from which D02HBF is called.

BC – SUBROUTINE, supplied by the user.

BC must place in G1 and G2 the boundary conditions at A and B respectively (see RANGE below).

Its specification is:

```
SUBROUTINE BC(G1, G2, P)
real       F1(n), G2(n), P(n1)
```

where n and n1 are the actual values of N and N1 in the call of D02HBF.

G1 – *real* array of DIMENSION (n).

On exit, G1(i) must contain the value of $y_i(A)$, (where this may be a known value or a function of the parameters $P(j)$, $j = 1,2,...,n1$), for $i = 1,2,...,n$.

G2 – *real* array of DIMENSION (n).

On exit, G2(i) must contain the value of $y_i(B)$, for $i = 1,2,...,n$, (where these may be known values or functions of the parameters $P(j)$, $j = 1,2,...,n1$). If $N > N1$, so that there are some driving equations, then the first $N - N1$ values of G2 need not be set since they are never used.

P – *real* array of DIMENSION (n1).

On entry, P(i) contains an estimate of the i(th) parameter, for $i = 1,2,...,n1$.

These values must not be changed.

BC must be declared as EXTERNAL in the (sub)program from which D02HBF is called.

RANGE – SUBROUTINE, supplied by the user.

RANGE must evaluate the boundary points A and B, each of which may depend on the parameters $P(1),P(2),...,P(N1)$. The integrations in the shooting method are always from A to B.

Its specification is:

```
SUBROUTINE RANGE(A, B, P)
real        A, B, P(n1)
```

where n1 is the actual value of N1 in the call of D02HBF.

A – *real*.

On exit, A must contain one of the boundary points.

B – *real*.

On exit, B must contain the second boundary point. Note that $B > A$ forces the direction of integration to be that of increasing X. If A and B are interchanged the direction of integration is reversed.

P – *real* array of DIMENSION (n1).

On entry, P(i) contains the current estimate of the i(th) parameter, for $i = 1,2,...,n1$.

These values must not be changed.

RANGE must be declared as EXTERNAL in the (sub)program from which D02HBF is called.

W – *real* array of DIMENSION (N,IW).

Used mainly as workspace.

On an error exit with IFAIL = 2, 3, 4 or 5 (see Section 6), W(I,1), I = 1,...,N contains the solution at the point X when the error occurred. W(1,2) contains X.

IW – INTEGER.

On entry, IW must specify the second dimension of the array W.

IW $\geq$ 3N + 14 + max(11,N).

Unchanged on exit.

IFAIL – INTEGER.

For this routine, the normal use of IFAIL is extended to control the printing of error messages and monitoring information as well as specifying hard or soft failure (see the Introduction to this Handbook).

Before entry, IFAIL must be set to a value with the decimal expansion cba, where each of the decimal digits c, b and a must have the value 0 or 1.

a = 0   specifies hard failure, otherwise soft failure;

b = 0   suppresses error messages, otherwise error messages will be printed (see Section 6);

c = 0   suppresses monitoring information, otherwise monitoring information will be printed.

The recommended value for inexperienced users is 110 (i.e. hard failure with all error messages and monitoring information printed).

Unless the routine detects an error (see Section 6), IFAIL contains 0 on exit.

## 6. Error Indicators and Warnings

Errors detected by the routine:

For each error, the routine outputs an explanatory error message on the current error message unit (see NAG Workstation Library routine X04AAF), unless suppressed by the value of IFAIL on entry.

IFAIL = 1

One or more of the parameters N, N1, M1, IW, E or PE is incorrectly set.

IFAIL = 2

The step-length for the integration became too short whilst calculating the residual (see Section 8).

IFAIL = 3

No initial step-length could be chosen for the integration whilst calculating the residual.

**Note**: IFAIL = 2 or 3 can occur due to choosing too small values for the elements of E or due to choosing the wrong direction of integration. Try varying E and interchanging A and B. These error exits can also occur for very poor initial choices of the parameters in the array P and, in extreme cases, because this routine cannot be used to solve the problem posed.

IFAIL = 4

As for IFAIL = 2 but the error occurred when calculating the Jacobian.

IFAIL = 5

As for IFAIL = 3 but the error occurred when calculating the Jacobian.

IFAIL = 6

The calculated Jacobian has an insignificant column. This can occur because a parameter P(I) is incorrectly entered when posing the problem.

**Note**: IFAIL = 4, 5 or 6 usually indicate a badly scaled problem. The user may vary the size of the elements of PE. Otherwise the use of the more general routine D02SAF which affords more control over the calculations is advised.

IFAIL = 7

The linear algebra routine (F02SZF) used internally has failed. This error exit should not occur and can be avoided by changing the initial estimates P(I).

IFAIL = 8

The Newton iteration has failed to converge having tried all iterates available to it. This can indicate a poor initial choice of parameters P(I) or a very difficult problem. Consider varying the elements PE(I) if the residuals are small in the monitoring output. If the residuals are large, try varying the initial parameters P(I).

IFAIL = 9
IFAIL = 10
IFAIL = 11
IFAIL = 12
IFAIL = 13

A serious error has occurred in an internal call to the auxiliary routine D02SAZ, D02SAW, D02SAX, D02SAU or D02SAV respectively. Check all array subscripts and subroutine parameter lists in call to D02HBF. Seek expert help.

## 7. Accuracy

If the process converges, the accuracy to which the unknown parameters are determined is usually close to that specified by the user; and the solution, if requested, may be determined to a required accuracy by varying the parameter E.

## 8. Further Comments

Timing depends on the complexity of the system, and on the number of iterations required. In practice, integration of the differential equations is by far the most costly process involved.

Wherever they occur in the routine, the error parameters contained in the arrays E and PE are used in 'mixed' form; that is $E(I)$ always occurs in expressions of the form

$$E(I) \times (1 + abs(y(I)))$$

and $PE(I)$ always occurs in expressions of the form

$$PE(I) \times (1 + abs(P(I)))$$

Though not ideal for every application, it is expected that this mixture of absolute and relative error testing will be adequate for most purposes.

The best direction of integration is usually the direction of decreasing solutions. The user is strongly recommended to set IFAIL to obtain self-explanatory error messages, and also monitoring information about the course of the computation. The user may select the channel numbers on which this output is to appear by calls of X04AAF (for error messages) or X04ABF (for monitoring information) – see Section 9 for an example. Otherwise the default channel numbers will be used, as specified in the appropriate Appendix. The monitoring information produced at each iteration includes the current parameter values, the residuals and two norms: a basic norm and a current norm. At each iteration the aim is to find parameter values which make the current norm less than the basic norm. Both these norms should tend to zero as should the residuals. (They would all be zero if the exact parameters were used as input.) For more details, in particular about the other monitoring information printed, the user is advised to consult the specification of routine D02SAF and, especially, the description of the parameter MONIT there.

The computing time for integrating the differential equations can sometimes depend critically on the quality of the initial estimates for the parameters $P(I)$. If it seems that too much computing time is required and, in particular, if the values of the residuals printed by the monitoring routine are much larger than the expected values of the solution at B then the coding of the subroutines FCN, BC and RANGE should be checked for errors. If no errors can be found, an independent attempt should be made to improve the initial estimates for $P(I)$.

The subroutine can be used to solve a very wide range of problems, for example:

(1) eigenvalue problems, including problems where the eigenvalue occurs in the boundary conditions;

(2) problems where the differential equations depend on some parameters which are to be determined so as to satisfy certain boundary conditions (see example (ii) in Section 9);

(3) problems where one of the end-points of the range of integration is to be determined as the point where a variable $Y(I)$ takes a particular value (see example (ii) in Section 9);

(4) singular problems and problems on infinite ranges of integration where the values of the solution at A or B or both are determined by a power series or an asymptotic expansion (or a more complicated expression) and where some of the coefficients in the expression are to be determined (see example (i) in Section 9);

(5) differential equations with certain terms defined by other independent (driving) differential equations.

Subroutine D02HBF uses labelled COMMON blocks AD02HB, AD02SA and BD02SA.

# E02BAF

## 1. Purpose

E02BAF computes a weighted least-squares approximation to an arbitrary set of data points by a cubic spline with knots prescribed by the user. Cubic spline interpolation can also be carried out.

## 2. Specification

```
      SUBROUTINE E02BAF (M, NCAP7, X, Y, W, K, WORK1, WORK2, C, SS,
     1                   IFAIL)
C     INTEGER    M, NCAP7, IFAIL
C     real       X(M), Y(M), W(M), K(NCAP7), WORK1(M),
     1           WORK2(4,NCAP7), C(NCAP7), SS
```

## 3. Description

This routine determines a least-squares cubic-spline approximation $S(X)$ to the set of data points $(X(R),Y(R))$ with weights $W(R)$ $(R = 1,2,...,M)$. The value of $NCAP7 = NCAP + 7$, where NCAP is the number of intervals of the spline (one greater than the number of interior knots), and the values of the knots $K(5),K(6),...,K(NCAP+3)$, interior to the data interval, are prescribed by the user.

$S(X)$ has the property that it minimizes SS, the sum of the squares of the weighted residuals $EPS(R)$ $(R = 1,2,...,M)$, where

$\quad EPS(R) = W(R) \times (S(X(R))-Y(R))$.

The routine produces one minimizing value of SS and the coefficients $C(1),C(2),...,C(Q)$, where $Q = NCAP + 3$, in the B-spline representation

$\quad S(X) = C(1) \times N1(X)+C(2) \times N2(X) + ... + C(Q) \times NQ(X)$

Here $NI(X)$ $(I = 1,2,...,Q)$ denotes the normalised B-spline of degree 3 defined upon the knots $K(I)$, $K(I+1)$, $K(I+2)$, $K(I+3)$ and $K(I+4)$.

In order to define the full set of B-splines required, eight additional knots $K(1)$, $K(2)$, $K(3)$, $K(4)$, $K(NCAP+4)$, $K(NCAP+5)$, $K(NCAP+6)$ and $K(NCAP+7)$ are inserted automatically by the routine. The first four of these are set equal to the smallest $X(R)$ and the last four to the largest $X(R)$.

The representation of $S(X)$ in terms of B-splines is the most compact form possible in that only $NCAP+3$ coefficients, in addition to the $NCAP+7$ knots, fully define $S(X)$.

The method employed involves forming and then computing the least-squares solution of a set of M linear equations in the coefficients C(I) (I = 1,2,...,NCAP+3). The equations are formed using a recurrence relation for B-splines that is unconditionally stable ([1], [5]), even for multiple (coincident) knots. The least-squares solution is also obtained in a stable manner by using orthogonal transformations, viz. a variant of Givens rotations ([6], [7]). This requires only one equation to be stored at a time. Full advantage is taken of the structure of the equations, there being at most four non-zero values of NI(X) for any value of X and hence at most four coefficients in each equation.

For further details of the algorithm and its use see [2], [3] and [4].

Subsequent evaluation of S(X) from its B-spline representation may be carried out using the NAG Workstation Library routine E02BBF. If derivatives of S(X) are also required, the NAG Workstation Library routine E02BCF may be used. NAG Workstation Library routine E02BDF can be used to compute the definite integral of S(X).

## 4. References

[1]  COX, M.G.
The numerical evaluation of B-splines.
J. Inst. Maths. Applics., 10, pp. 134-149, 1972.

[2]  COX, M.G.
A data-fitting package for the non-specialist user.
In Software for Numerical Mathematics. Evans, D.J. (ed.)
Academic Press, London, 1974.

[3]  COX, M.G.
Numerical methods for the interpolation and approximation of data by spline functions.
PhD Thesis, City University, London, 1975.

[4]  COX, M.G. and HAYES, J.G.
Curve Fitting: a Guide and Suite of Algorithms for the Non-Specialist User.
Report NAC26, National Physical Laboratory, Teddington, Middlesex, 1973.

[5]  DE BOOR, C.
On calculating with B-splines.
J. Approx. Theory, 6, pp. 50-62, 1972.

[6]  GENTLEMAN, W.M.
Algorithm AS 75.
Basic procedures for large sparse or weighted linear least-squares problems.
Appl. Statist. 23, pp. 448-454, 1974.

[7]  GENTLEMAN, W.M.
     Least-squares computations by Givens transformations without square roots.
     J. Inst. Maths. Applics. 12, pp. 329-336, 1973.

[8]  SCHOENBERG, I.J. and WHITNEY, Anne.
     On Polya frequency functions III, pp. 246-259.
     Trans. Amer. Math. Soc. 74, 1953.

## 5. Parameters

M – INTEGER.

On entry, M must specify the number of data points.

$M \geq MDIST \geq 4$, where MDIST is the number of distinct X values in the data.

Unchanged on exit.

NCAP7 – INTEGER.

On entry, NCAP7 must specify NCAP+7, where NCAP is the number of intervals of the spline (which is one greater than the number of interior knots, i.e. the knots strictly within the range $X(1)$ to $X(M)$) over which the spline is defined.

$8 \leq NCAP7 \leq MDIST+4$, where MDIST is the number of distinct X values in the data.

Unchanged on exit.

X – *real* array of DIMENSION at least (M).

Before entry, $X(R)$ must be set to the R(th) value of the independent variable (abscissa) X, for R = 1,2,...,M.
These values must be supplied in non-decreasing order.

Unchanged on exit.

Y – *real* array of DIMENSION at least (M).

Before entry, $Y(R)$ must be set to the R(th) value of the dependent variable (ordinate) Y, for R = 1,2,...,M.

Unchanged on exit.

W – *real* array of DIMENSION at least (M).

Before entry, $W(R)$ must be set to the R(th) value in the set of weights, for R = 1,2,...,M. The $W(R)$ must be strictly positive. For advice on the choice of weights, see the Chapter Introduction.

Unchanged on exit.

K – **real** array of DIMENSION at least (NCAP7).

Before entry, K(I) must be set to the (I−4)th (interior) knot, for I = 5,6,...,NCAP+3. The knots must be in non-decreasing order and lie strictly between X(1) and X(M).

On exit, these values are unchanged, and K(I), for I = 1,2,3,4, NCAP+4, NCAP+5, NCAP+6 and NCAP+7, contain the additional (exterior) knots introduced by the routine. For advice on the choice of knots, see the Chapter Introduction.

WORK1 – **real** array of DIMENSION at least (M).

Used as working space.

WORK2 – **real** array of DIMENSION at least (4∗NCAP7).

Used as working space.

C – **real** array of DIMENSION at least (NCAP7).

On successful exit, C(I) contains the coefficient of the B-spline NI(X), for I = 1,2,...,NCAP+3. The remaining elements of the array are not used.

SS – **real**.

On successful exit, SS contains the residual sum of squares.

IFAIL – INTEGER.

Before entry, IFAIL must be set to 0 or 1. For users not familiar with this parameter (described in the Introduction to this Handbook) the recommended value is 0.

Unless the routine detects an error (see next section), IFAIL contains 0 on exit.

## 6. Error Indicators and Warnings

Errors detected by the routine:

IFAIL = 1

The knots fail to satisfy the condition
   X(1) < K(5) ≤ K(6) ≤ ... ≤ K(NCAP + 3) < X(M).
Thus the knots are not in correct order or are not interior to the data interval.

IFAIL = 2

The weights are not all strictly positive.

IFAIL = 3

The values of X(R) (R = 1,2,...,M) are not in non-decreasing order.

IFAIL = 4

NCAP7 < 8 (so the number of interior knots is negative) or NCAP7 > MDIST+4, where MDIST is the number of distinct X values in the data (so there cannot be a unique solution).

IFAIL = 5

The conditions specified by Schoenberg and Whitney [8] fail to hold for at least one subset of the distinct data abscissae. That is there is no subset of NCAP+3 strictly increasing values, X(R(1)),X(R(2)),...,X(R(NCAP+3)), among the abscissae such that

$$X(R(1)) < K(1) < X(R(5)),$$

$$X(R(2)) < K(2) < X(R(6)),$$

..........

$$X(R(NCAP-1)) < K(NCAP-1) < X(R(NCAP+3)).$$

This means that there is no unique solution: there are regions containing too many knots compared with the number of data points.

## 7. Accuracy

The rounding errors are such that the computed coefficients are exact for a slightly perturbed set of ordinates Y(R) + DELTAY(R). The ratio of the root-mean-square value for the DELTAY(R) to the root-mean-square value of the Y(R) can be expected to be less than a small multiple of cappa × M × EPS. Here EPS is the relative machine precision (see NAG Workstation Library routine X02AAF), and cappa is a condition number for the problem. Values of cappa for 20-30 practical data sets all proved to lie between 4.5 and 7.8 (see [3]). (Note that for these data sets, replacing the coincident end knots at the endpoints X(1) and X(M) used in the routine by various choices of non-coincident exterior knots gave values of cappa between 16 and 180. Again see [3] for further details.) In general we would not expect cappa to be large unless the choice of knots results in near-violation of the Schoenberg-Whitney conditions.

A cubic spline which adequately fits the data and is free from spurious oscillations is more likely to be obtained if the knots are chosen to be grouped more closely in regions where the function (underlying the data) or its derivatives change more rapidly than elsewhere.

## 8. Further Comments

The time taken is approximately proportional to $2 \times M + NCAP7$.

Multiple knots are permitted as long as their multiplicity does not exceed 4, i.e. the complete set of knots must satisfy $K(I) < K(I+4)$ $(I = 1,2,...,NCAP+3)$ (cf Section 6). At a knot of multiplicity one (the usual case), $S(X)$ and its first two derivative are continuous. At a knot of multiplicity two, $S(X)$ and its first derivative are continuous. At a knot of multiplicity three, $S(X)$ is continuous, and at a knot of multiplicity four, $S(X)$ is generally discontinous.

The routine can be used efficiently for cubic spline interpolation, i.e. if $M = NCAP+3$. The abscissae must then of course satisfy $X(1) < X(2) < ... < X(M)$. Recommended values for the knots in this case are $K(I) = X(I-2)$ $(I = 5,6,...,NCAP+3)$.

# E02BCF

## 1. Purpose

E02BCF evaluates a cubic spline and its first three derivatives from its B-spline representation.

## 2. Specification

```
      SUBROUTINE E02BCF (NCAP7, K, C, X, LEFT, S, IFAIL)
C     INTEGER     NCAP7, LEFT, IFAIL
C     real        K(NCAP7), C(NCAP7), X, S(4)
```

## 3. Description

This routine evaluates the cubic spline $S(X)$ and its first three derivatives at a prescribed argument X. It is assumed that $S(X)$ is represented in terms of its B-spline coefficients $C(I)$ ($I = 1,2,...,NCAP+3$) and (augmented) ordered knot set $K(I)$ ($I = 1,2,...,NCAP+7$) (see NAG Workstation Library routine E02BAF), i.e.

$$S(X) = C(1) \times N1(X) + C(2) \times N2(X) + ... + C(Q) \times NQ(X).$$

Here $Q = NCAP+3$, NCAP is the number of intervals of the spline and $NI(X)$ denotes the normalised B-spline [2] of degree 3 (order 4) defined upon the knots $K(I)$, $K(I+1)$, $K(I+2)$, $K(I+3)$ and $K(I+4)$. The prescribed argument X must satisfy

$$K(4) \leq X \leq K(NCAP+4).$$

At a simple knot $K(I)$ (i.e. one satisfying $K(I-1) < K(I) < K(I+1)$), the third derivative of the spline is in general discontinuous. At a multiple knot (i.e. two or more knots with the same value), lower derivatives, and even the spline itself, may be discontinuous. Specifically, at a point $X = U$ where (exactly) r knots coincide (such a point is termed a knot of multiplicity r), the values of the derivatives of order $4 - j$, for $j = 1,2,...,r$, are in general discontinuous. (Here $1 \leq r \leq 4; r > 4$ is not meaningful.) The user must specify whether the value at such a point is required to be the left- or right-hand derivative.

The method employed is based upon:

   (i) carrying out a binary search for the knot interval containing the argument X (see [3]),

  (ii) evaluating the non-zero B-splines of orders 1,2,3 and 4 by recurrence (see [2], [3]),

 (iii) computing all derivatives of the B-splines of order 4 by applying a second recurrence to these computed B-spline values (see [1]),

(iv)  multiplying the 4th-order B-spline values and their derivative by the appropriate B-spline coefficients, and summing, to yield the values of S(X) and its derivatives.

E02BCF can be used to compute the values and derivatives of cubic spline fits and interpolants produced by the NAG Workstation Library routine E02BAF.

If only values and not derivatives are required, the NAG Workstation Library routine E02BBF may be used instead of E02BCF, which takes about 50% longer than E02BBF.

## 4. References

[1]  DE BOOR, C.
     On Calculating with B-splines.
     J. Approx. Theory, 6, pp. 50-62, 1972.

[2]  COX, M.G.
     The numerical evaluation of B-splines.
     J. Inst. Maths. Applics., 10, pp. 134-149, 1972.

[3]  COX, M.G.
     The numerical evaluation of a spline from its B-spline representation.
     J. Inst. Maths. Applics., 21, pp. 135-143, 1978.

## 5. Parameters

NCAP7 – INTEGER.

On entry, NCAP7 must specify NCAP + 7, where NCAP is the number of intervals of the spline (which is one greater than the number of interior knots, i.e. the knots strictly within the range K(4) to K(NCAP+4)) over which the spline is defined.

NCAP7 $\geq$ 8.

Unchanged on exit.

K – *real* array of DIMENSION at least (NCAP7).

Before entry, K(J) must be set to the value of the J(th) member of the complete set of knots, for J = 1,2,...,NCAP7. The K(J) must be in non-decreasing order with K(NCAP+4) > K(4).

Unchanged on exit.

C – *real* array of DIMENSION at least (NCAP7).

Before entry, C(J) must be set to the value of the J(th) B-spline coefficient, for J = 1,2,...,NCAP+3. The remaining elements of the array are not used.

Unchanged on exit.

X – *real*.

On entry, X must specify the argument at which the cubic spline and its derivatives are to be evaluated.

$K(4) \leq X \leq K(NCAP+4)$.

Unchanged on exit.

LEFT – INTEGER.

On entry, LEFT must specify whether left- or right-hand values of the spline and its derivatives are to be computed (see Section 3). Left- or right-hand values are formed according to whether LEFT is equal or not equal to 1. If X does not coincide with a knot, the value of LEFT is immaterial. If $X = K(4)$, right-hand values are computed, and if $X = K(NCAP+4)$, left-hand values are formed, regardless of the value of LEFT.

Unchanged on exit.

S – *real* array of DIMENSION at least (4).

On successful exit, S(J) contains the value of the $(J-1)$th derivative of the spline at the argument X, for $J = 1,2,3,4$.

Note that S(1) contains the value of the spline.

IFAIL – INTEGER.

Before entry, IFAIL must be set to 0 or 1. For users not familiar with this parameter (described in the Introduction to this Handbook) the recommended value is 0.

Unless the routine detects an error (see next section), IFAIL contains 0 on exit.

## 6. Error Indicators and Warnings

Errors detected by the routine:

IFAIL = 1

$NCAP7 < 8$, i.e. the number of intervals is not positive.

IFAIL = 2

Either $K(4) \geq K(NCAP+4)$, i.e. the range over which S(X) is defined is null or negative in length, or X is an invalid argument, i.e. $K(NCAP+4) < X < K(4)$.

## 7. Accuracy

The computed value of S(X) has negligible error in most practical situations. Specifically, this value has an **absolute** error bounded in modulus by $18 \times CMAX \times EPS$, where CMAX is the largest in modulus of C(J), C(J+1), C(J+2) and C(J+3), J is an integer such that $K(J+3) \leq X \leq K(J+4)$, and EPS is the relative machine precision (see NAG Workstation Library routine X02AAF). If C(J), C(J+1), C(J+2) and C(J+3) are all of the same sign, then the computed value of S(X) has **relative** error bounded by 18×EPS. For full details see [3].

No complete error analysis is available for the computation of the derivatives of S(X). However, for most practical purposes the absolute errors in the computed derivatives should be small.

## 8. Further Comments

The time taken is approximately linear in log(NCAP7).

IMPORTANT: The routine does not test all the conditions on the knots given in the description of K in Section 5, since to do this would result in a computation time approximately linear in NCAP7 instead of log(NCAP7). All the conditions are tested in E02BAF, however.

# E02BDF

## 1. Purpose

E02BDF computes the definite integral of a cubic spline from its B-spline representation.

## 2. Specification

```
      SUBROUTINE E02BDF (NCAP7, K, C, DEFINT, IFAIL)
C     INTEGER    NCAP7, IFAIL
C     real       K(NCAP7), C(NCAP7), DEFINT
```

## 3. Description

This routine computes the definite integral of the cubic spline $S(X)$ between the limits $X = A$ and $X = B$, where A and B are respectively the lower and upper limits of the range over which $S(X)$ is defined. It is assumed that $S(X)$ is represented in terms of its B-spline coefficients $C(I)$ $(I = 1,2,...,NCAP+3)$ and (augmented) ordered knot set $K(I)$ $(I = 1,2,...,NCAP+7)$ with $K(I) = A$ for $I = 1,2,3,4$ and $K(I) = B$ for $I = NCAP+4, NCAP+5, NCAP+6, NCAP+7$ (see E02BAF), i.e.

$$S(X) = C(1) \times N1(X) + C(2) \times N2(X) + ... + C(Q) \times NQ(X).$$

Here $Q = NCAP+3$, NCAP is the number of intervals of the spline and $NI(X)$ denotes the normalised B-spline [1] of degree 3 (order 4) defined upon the knots $K(I)$, $K(I+1)$, $K(I+2)$, $K(I+3)$ and $K(I+4)$.

The method employed uses the formula given in Section 3 of [1].

E02BDF can be used to determine the definite integrals of cubic spline fits and interpolants produced by the NAG Workstation Library routine E02BAF.

## 4. References

[1] COX, M.G.
     An algorithm for spline interpolation.
     J. Inst. Maths. Applics., 15, pp. 95-108, 1975.

## 5. Parameters

NCAP7 – INTEGER.

On entry, NCAP7 must specify NCAP + 7, where NCAP is the number of intervals of the spline (which is one greater than the number of interior knots, i.e. the knots strictly within the range A to B) over which the spline is defined.

NCAP7 ≥ 8.

Unchanged on exit.

K – *real* array of DIMENSION at least (NCAP7).

Before entry, K(J) must be set to the value of the J(th) member of the complete set of knots, for J = 1,2,...,NCAP7. The K(J) must be in non-decreasing order with K(NCAP+4) > K(4) and satisfy

$$K(1) = K(2) = K(3) = K(4)$$

and

$$K(NCAP+4) = K(NCAP+5) = K(NCAP+6) = K(NCAP7).$$

Unchanged on exit.

C – *real* array of DIMENSION at least (NCAP7).

Before entry, C(J) must be set to the value of the J(th) B-spline coefficient, for J = 1,2,...,NCAP+3. The remaining elements of the array are not used.

Unchanged on exit.

DEFINT – *real*.

On successful exit, DEFINT contains the value of the definite integral of S(X) between the limits X = A and X = B, where A = K(4) and B = K(NCAP+4).

IFAIL – INTEGER.

Before entry, IFAIL must be set to 0 or 1. For users not familiar with this parameter (described in the Introduction to this Handbook) the recommended value is 0.

Unless the routine detects an error (see next section), IFAIL contains 0 on exit.

## 6. Error Indicators and Warnings

Errors detected by the routine:

IFAIL = 1

NCAP7 < 8, i.e. the number of intervals is not positive.

IFAIL = 2

At least one of the following restrictions on the knots is violated:
K(NCAP+4) > K(4), K(J) ≥ K(J−1) (J = 2,3,...,NCAP7), with equality
in the cases J = 2,3,4, NCAP+5, NCAP+6 and NCAP7.

## 7. Accuracy

The rounding errors are such that the computed value of the integral is exact
for a slightly perturbed set of B-spline coefficients C(I) differing in a relative
sense from those supplied by no more than $2.2 \times (NCAP+3) \times EPS$, where
EPS is the relative machine precision (see NAG Workstation Library routine
X02AAF).

## 8. Further Comments

The time taken is approximately proportional to NCAP7.

# E04VDF

## 1. Purpose

E04VDF is an easy-to-use routine designed to minimize an arbitrary smooth function subject to constraints, which may include simple bounds on the variables, linear constraints and smooth nonlinear constraints. ( E04VDF may also be used for unconstrained, bound-constrained and linearly constrained optimization.) The user must provide subroutines that define the objective and constraint functions and their gradients. All matrices are treated as dense, and hence E04VDF is not intended for large sparse problems.

## 2. Specification

```
      SUBROUTINE E04VDF (ITMAX, MSGLVL, N, NCLIN, NCNLN, NCTOTL,
     1                   NROWA, NROWJ, CTOL, FTOL, A, BL, BU, CONFUN, OBJFUN,
     2                   X, ISTATE, C, CJAC, OBJF, OBJGRD, CLAMDA, IWORK,
     3                   LIWORK, WORK, LWORK, IFAIL)
C     EXTERNAL     CONFUN, OBJFUN
C     INTEGER      ITMAX, MSGLVL, N, NCLIN, NCNLN, NCTOTL, NROWA, NROWJ,
C     1            LIWORK, LWORK, IFAIL, ISTATE(NCTOTL), IWORK(LIWORK)
C     real         CTOL, FTOL, OBJF, A(NROWA,N), BL(NCTOTL),
C     1            BU(NCTOTL), X(N), C(NROWJ), CJAC(NROWJ,N),
C     2            CLAMDA(NCTOTL), OBJGRD(N), WORK(LWORK)
```

## 3. Description

E04VDF solves nonlinear programming (NP) problems of the form

$$\underset{x \in R^n}{\text{minimize}} \ F(x) \qquad \text{subject to } \ell \le \left\{ \begin{array}{c} x \\ Ax \\ c(x) \end{array} \right\} \le u,$$

where $F(x)$ is a smooth nonlinear function, A is a constant matrix and $c(x)$ is a vector of smooth nonlinear constraint functions. The matrix A and/or the vector $c(x)$ may be empty. Note that upper and lower bounds are specified for all the variables and for all the constraints. This form allows full generality in specifying other types of constraints. For example, the i(th) constraint may be specified as equality by setting $\ell_i = u_i$. If certain bounds are not present, the associated elements of $\ell$ or u can be set to special values that will be treated as $-\infty$ or $+\infty$.

The user must supply an initial estimate of the solution together with subroutines that define $F(x)$, $c(x)$ and their first derivatives.

E04VDF implements a sequential quadratic programming method in which the search direction is the solution of a quadrature programming problem. Further details can be found in references [1] and [2].

## 4. References

[1]  GILL, P.E., MURRAY, W. and WRIGHT, M.H.
Practical Optimization.
Academic Press, London, 1981.

[2]  GILL, P.E., MURRAY, W., SAUNDERS, M.A. and WRIGHT, M.H.
User's Guide for SOL/NPSOL: A Fortran Package for Nonlinear Programming. Report SOL 83-12.
Department of Operations Research, Stanford University, California 94305, USA, 1983.

## 5. Parameters

### 5.1. Input Parameters

ITMAX – INTEGER.

On entry, ITMAX must specify an upper bound on the number of iterations to be taken. Unless the problem is known to be very difficult, a sensible initial choice for ITMAX is 50. If ITMAX is not positive then the value 50 is used in place of ITMAX.

Unchanged on exit.

MSGLVL – INTEGER.

On entry, MSGLVL must specify whether or not printout is required at the final solution. When printing occurs the output is on the advisory message channel (see NAG Workstation Library routine X04ABF). A description of the printed output is given in Section 5.6. The level of printing is determined as follows.

MSGLVL $< 0$

No printing.

MSGLVL $= 0$

Printing **only** if an input parameter is incorrect, or if the working set is so ill-conditioned that subsequent overflow is likely. This setting is strongly recommended in preference to MSGLVL $< 0$.

MSGLVL $= 1$

Printing at the solution.

MSGLVL $> 1$

Values greater than 1 should normally be used **only** at the direction of NAG Central Office; such values may generate large amounts of printed output.

Unchanged on exit.

# INDEX

N – INTEGER.

On entry, N must specify the number of variables.

N ≥ 1.

Unchanged on exit.

NCLIN – INTEGER.

On entry, NCLIN must specify the number of general linear constraints in the problem.

NCLIN ≥ 0.

Unchanged on exit.

NCNLN – INTEGER.

On entry, NCNLN must specify the number of nonlinear constraints in the problem.

NCNLN ≥ 0.

Unchanged on exit.

NCTOTL – INTEGER.

On entry, NCTOTL must specify the value (N + NCLIN + NCNLN).

Unchanged on exit.

NROWA – INTEGER.

On entry, NROWA must specify the first dimension of A as declared in the (sub)program from which E04VDF is called.

NROWA ≥ max(1,NCLIN).

Unchanged on exit.

NROWJ – INTEGER.

On entry, NROWJ must specify the first dimension of the array CJAC as declared in the (sub)program from which E04VDF is called.

NROWJ ≥ max(1,NCNLN).

Unchanged on exit.

CTOL – *real*.

On entry, CTOL must specify an absolute tolerance that defines the maximum permissible violation in a constraint in order for a point to be considered feasible. As CTOL increases, the algorithm used by E04VDF is less likely to encounter difficulties with ill-conditioning and degeneracy. However larger values of CTOL mean that a constraint could be violated by a significant amount. If the constraints are well scaled, then $\sqrt{eps}$, where eps is the machine precision (see NAG Workstation Library routine X02AAF), is often a reasonable choice. If CTOL is supplied as less than eps, then a value of approximately $\sqrt{\text{eps}}$ will be used in place of CTOL.

Unchanged on exit.

**FTOL** – *real*.

On entry, FTOL must specify a positive relative tolerance that indicates the number of figures of accuracy desired in the objective function at the solution. For example, if FTOL is $10^{-6}$ and E04VDF terminates successfully, the computed solution should have approximately six correct figures in F. If FTOL is supplied as less than eps, where eps is the machine precision (see NAG Workstation Library routine X02AAF), then the value eps will be used in place of FTOL.

Unchanged on exit.

**A** – *real* array of DIMENSION (NROWA,nca), where nca $\geq$ N.

Before entry, the leading NCLIN-by-N part of A must contain the NCLIN general linear constraints, with the coefficients of the i(th) constraint in the i(th) row of A. If NCLIN $=$ 0, then A is not referenced.

Unchanged on exit.

**BL** – *real* array of DIMENSION at least (NCTOTL).

Before entry, the first N elements of BL must contain the lower bounds on the N variables; when NCLIN $>$ 0, the next NCLIN elements of BL must contain the lower bounds on the NCLIN general linear constraints; and when NCNLN $>$ 0, the next NCNLN elements of BL must contain the lower bounds on the NCNLN nonlinear constraints. To specify a non-existent lower bound ($\ell_j = -\infty$) set BL(j) $\leq$ –1.0E + 20.

Unchanged on exit.

**BU** – *real* array of DIMENSION at least (NCTOTL).

Before entry, the elements of BU must contain the upper bounds on the variables and constraints in the order described above for BL. To specify a non-existent upper bound ($u_j = +\infty$) set BU(j) $\geq$ 1.0E + 20.

BU(j) $\geq$ BL(j), j $=$ 1,2,...,NCTOTL.

Unchanged on exit.

**CONFUN** – SUBROUTINE, supplied by the user.

CONFUN must return the values of the vector of nonlinear constraint functions, c(x), and its Jacobian for a given n element vector x. When NCNLN $=$ 0, then CONFUN is not referenced by E04VDF and CONFUN may be the dummy routine E04VDM. (E04VDM is included in the NAG Workstation Library and so need not be supplied by the user. Its name may be implementation-dependent: see the appropriate Appendix for details.) When NCNLN $> 0$, then E04VDF always calls CONFUN and OBJFUN together in that order.

Its specification is:

```
SUBROUTINE CONFUN (MODE, NCNLN, N, NROWJ, X, C, CJAC, NSTATE)
INTEGER    MODE, NCNLN, N, NROWJ, NSTATE
real       X(N), C(NROWJ), CJAC(NROWJ,N)
```

MODE – INTEGER.

MODE is a flag that the user may set within CONFUN to indicate a failure in the evaluation of the nonlinear constraints, or their derivatives. On entry, MODE is always non-negative.

If MODE is negative on exit from CONFUN, the execution of E04VDF will be terminated with IFAIL set to MODE.

NCNLN – INTEGER.

On entry, NCNLN specifies the number of nonlinear constraints as input to E04VDF.

NCNLN must not be altered by CONFUN.

N – INTEGER.

On entry, N specifies the number of variables as input to E04VDF.

N must not be altered by CONFUN.

NROWJ – INTEGER.

On entry, NROWJ specifies the first dimension of CJAC and the length of the array C as input to E04VDF.

NROWJ must not be altered by CONFUN.

X – *real* array of DIMENSION (N).

On entry, X contains the vector of variables, x, at which the constraint functions are to be evaluated.

X must not be altered by CONFUN.

C – *real* array of DIMENSION (NROWJ).

On exit, C must contain the NCNLN nonlinear constraint values, with the value of the j(th) nonlinear constraint in C(j).

CJAC – *real* array of DIMENSION (NROWJ,N).

On exit, CJAC must contain the NCNLN-by-N Jacobian of the constraint functions with the i(th) row of CJAC containing the gradient of the i(th) nonlinear constraint. Thus CJAC(i,j) must contain the partial derivative of $c_i$ with respect to $x_j$. If CJAC contains any constant elements, then a saving in computation can be made by setting them once only when NSTATE = 1 (see below).

### NSTATE – INTEGER.

On entry, NSTATE will be 1 on the first call to CONFUN by E04VDF and is 0 on all subsequent calls. Thus the user may test NSTATE within CONFUN in order to perform certain calculations or operations once only. For example, the user may wish to calculate constant elements, read data, or initialise COMMON blocks.

NSTATE must not be changed by CONFUN.

CONFUN must be declared as EXTERNAL in the (sub)program from which E04VDF is called. CONFUN should be tested separately before being used in conjunction with E04VDF and the use of the NAG Workstation Library routine E04ZCF to check the derivatives returned by CONFUN is strongly recommended.

### OBJFUN – SUBROUTINE, supplied by the user.

OBJFUN must return the value of the objective function $F(x)$ and its gradient for a given n element vector x. When NCNLN > 0 then CONFUN and OBJFUN are always called together in that order.

Its specification is:

```
SUBROUTINE OBJFUN (MODE, N, X, OBJF, OBJGRD, NSTATE)
INTEGER    MODE, N, NSTATE
real       X(N), OBJF, OBJGRD(N)
```

### MODE – INTEGER.

MODE is a flag that the user may set within OBJFUN to indicate a failure in the evaluation of the objective function, or its derivatives. On entry, MODE is always non-negative.

If MODE is negative on exit from OBJFUN, the execution of E04VDF will be terminated with IFAIL set to MODE.

### N – INTEGER.

On entry, N specifies the number of variables as input to E04VDF.

N must not be altered by OBJFUN.

### X – *real* array of DIMENSION (N).

On entry, X contains the vector of variables, x, at which the objective function is to be evaluated.

X must not be altered by OBJFUN.

OBJF – *real*.

On exit, OBJF must contain the value of the objective function.

OBJGRD – *real* array of DIMENSION (N).

On exit, OBJGRD must contain the gradient of the objective function, with OBJGRD(j) containing the partial derivative of F with respect to $x_j$.

NSTATE – INTEGER.

On entry, NSTATE will be 1 on the first call to OBJFUN by E04VDF and is 0 on all subsequent calls. Thus the user may test NSTATE within OBJFUN in order to perform certain calculations or operations once only. For example, the user may wish to calculate constant elements, read data, or initialise COMMON blocks. Note that when NCNLN > 0 then CONFUN is always called before OBJFUN.

NSTATE must not be changed by OBJFUN.

OBJFUN must be declared as EXTERNAL in the (sub)program from which E04VDF is called. OBJFUN should be tested separately before being used in conjunction with E04VDF, and the use of the NAG Workstation Library routine E04ZCF to check the derivatives returned by OBJFUN is strongly recommended.

### 5.2. Input/Output Parameters

X – *real* array of DIMENSION at least (N).

Before entry, X must contain an estimate of the solution.

On successful exit, X will contain a solution to the nonlinear programming problem. On exit with 0 < IFAIL ≤ 5, or with IFAIL < 0, X will return the point at which the routine terminated.

### 5.3. Output Parameters

ISTATE – INTEGER array of DIMENSION at least (NCTOTL).

On successful exit, or on exit with 0 < IFAIL ≤ 5, ISTATE indicates the status of each constraint with respect to the current prediction of the active set. The first N elements of ISTATE refer to the upper and lower bounds on the variables; when NCLIN > 0, the next NCLIN elements refer to the general linear constraints; and when NCNLN > 0, the next NCNLN elements refer to the nonlinear constraints. Their meaning is:

| ISTATE(j) | Meaning |
|---|---|
| –2 | The constraint (or its linearisation) violates its lower bound in a quadratic programming subproblem. |
| –1 | The constraint (or its linearisation) violates its upper bound in a quadratic programming subproblem. |
| 0 | The constraint is not in the predicted active set. |

| 1 | The inequality constraint is included in the predicted active set at its lower bound. |
| 2 | The inequality constraint is included in the predicted active set at its upper bound. |
| 3 | The constraint is included in the predicted active set as an equality. This value can only occur when BL(j) = BU(j). |

C – *real* array of DIMENSION at least (NROWJ).

On successful exit, or on exit with $0 < \text{IFAIL} \leq 5$, C contains the NCNLN nonlinear constraint values at the final point. When NCNLN = 0, then C is not referenced by E04VDF.

CJAC – *real* array of DIMENSION (NROWJ,ncolj), where ncolj $\geq$ N.

On successful exit, or on exit with $0 < \text{IFAIL} \leq 5$, CJAC contains the NCNLN by N Jacobian of the nonlinear constraint functions at the final point. When NCNLN = 0, then CJAC is not referenced by E04VDF.

OBJF – *real*.

On successful exit, or on exit with $0 < \text{IFAIL} \leq 5$, OBJF contains the value of the objective function at the final point.

OBJGRD – *real* array of DIMENSION at least (N).

On successful exit, or on exit with $0 < \text{IFAIL} \leq 5$, OBJGRD contains the N elements of the gradient of the objective function at the final point.

CLAMDA – *real* array of DIMENSION at least (NCTOTL).

On successful exit, or on exit with $0 < \text{IFAIL} \leq 5$, CLAMDA contains estimates of the Lagrange multipliers for each constraint with respect to the predicted active set at the final point. The ordering of the elements of CLAMDA is as described above for ISTATE. If ISTATE(j) = 0, then CLAMDA(j) should be zero. On successful exit, if ISTATE(j) = 1 then CLAMDA(j) should be non-negative and if ISTATE(j) = 2 then CLAMDA(j) should be non-positive.

### 5.4. Workspace Parameters

IWORK – INTEGER array of DIMENSION (LIWORK).

Used as workspace.

LIWORK – INTEGER.

On entry, LIWORK must specify the length of the array IWORK as declared in the (sub)program from which E04VDF is called.

LIWORK $\geq$ 3N + NCLIN + NCNLN.

Unchanged on exit.

WORK – *real* array of DIMENSION (LWORK).

Used as workspace.

LWORK – INTEGER.

On entry, LWORK must specify the length of the array WORK as declared in the (sub)program from which E04VDF is called.

If NCNLN $>$ 0 then

LWORK $\geq$ $3 \times N^2$ + N$\times$(NCON+13) + 7$\times$NCON + 12$\times$NCNLN + NCLIN + NROWA

where NCON = NCLIN + NCNLN

otherwise

LWORK $\geq$ $3 \times N^2$ + 13$\times$N + 5$\times$NCLIN + 3$\times$NCON + NROWA

where NCON = NROWA if NCLIN $>$ 0 and NCON = 1 if NCLIN = 0.

When MSGLVL = 1 the amount of workspace provided and the amount of workspace required will be printed. As an alternative to evaluating the values for LIWORK and LWORK from the above formulae, the user may prefer to obtain the values from the output of a preliminary run with LIWORK = 1 and LWORK = 1.

Unchanged on exit.

### 5.5. Diagnostic Parameter

IFAIL – INTEGER.

Before entry, IFAIL must be set to 0 or 1. Users who are unfamiliar with this parameter should refer to the Introduction to this Handbook. IFAIL contains 0 on exit if X satisfies the first order optimality conditions.

**For this routine,** because the values of the output parameters may be useful even if IFAIL $\neq$ 0 on exit, users are recommended to set IFAIL to 1 before entry. **It is then essential to test the value of IFAIL on exit.**

### 5.6. Description of the printed output

Errors detected by the routine:

When MSGLVL = 1, then E04VDF will produce output on the current advisory message channel (see NAG Workstation Library routine X04ABF) giving information on the final point. The following describes the printout associated with each variable.

| Output | Meaning |
|--------|---------|
| VARBL | The name (V) and index j, j = 1,2,...,N of the variable. |
| STATE | The state of the variable. (FR if neither bound is in the working set, EQ for a fixed variable in the working set, LL if in the working set on its lower bound and UL if in the working set on its upper bound.) If the value of the variable lies outside the upper or lower bound then ISTATE will be '+ +' or '− −' respectively. |
| VALUE | The value of the variable at the final iteration. |
| LOWER BOUND | The lower bound specified for the variable. |
| UPPER BOUND | The upper bound specified for the variable. |
| LAGR MULT | The estimate of the Lagrange multiplier for the associated bound. |
| RESIDUAL | The difference between the value of the variable and the nearer of its bounds. |

For each of the constraints the printout is as above with variable replaced by constraint, except that for the general linear constraints VARBL is replaced by:

| LNCON | The name (L) and index j, j = 1,2,...,NCLIN, of the constraint. |
|-------|------|

and for the nonlinear constraints VARBL is replaced by

| NLCON | The name (N) and index j, j = 1,2,...,NCNLN, of the constraint. |
|-------|------|

## 6. Error Indicators and Warnings

Note:   When MSGLVL = 1 a short description of the error is printed.

IFAIL < 0

The user has set MODE to this negative value in either CONFUN or OBJFUN.

IFAIL = 1

No feasible point could be found for the linear constraints and bounds. The most likely reason for this condition is that the linear constraints and bounds are incompatible or inconsistent, in which case E04VDF will have terminated on the first iteration.

IFAIL = 2

The routine cannot improve upon the final point. This may be due to an overly stringent requested accuracy, that is FTOL is too small, in which case the final point may be acceptable despite the non-zero value of IFAIL.

IFAIL = 3

The limit of **ITMAX** iterations has been reached.

IFAIL = 4

Extremely small Lagrange multipliers could not be resolved. It may be possible to avoid the difficulty by removing certain active constraints with very small multipliers from the problem.

IFAIL = 5

A direction of descent could not be found. The computed gradients may be incorrect and the user should check that CONFUN and OBJFUN are working correctly. NAG Workstation Library routine E04ZCF can be used to check the computed derivatives.

IFAIL = 6

An input parameter is invalid. Unless MSGLVL $< 0$ a message will be printed.

Overflow

If the printed output before the overflow occurred contains a warning about serious ill-conditioning in the working set when adding the j(th) constraint then the offending linearly dependent constraint should be removed from the problem.

## 7. Accuracy

If IFAIL $= 0$ on exit, then the vector returned in the array X is an estimate of a solution to an accuracy of approximately $\sqrt{\text{FTOL}}$.

## 8. Further Comments

The time taken by the routine depends upon the number of variables, the behaviour of $F(x)$ and $c(x)$, the accuracy requested and the distance of the starting point from the solution. Each iteration makes at least one call to CONFUN and OBJFUN.

Sensible scaling of the objective function and constraints will reduce the difficulty of the problem so that E04VDF will take less computer time. See the Chapter Introduction and reference [1] for additional information and advice.

# F01BTF

## 1. Purpose

F01BTF decomposes a real matrix into a product of triangular matrices LU by Gaussian elimination with partial pivoting.

## 2. Specification

```
      SUBROUTINE F01BTF (N, A, IA, P, DP, IFAIL)
C     INTEGER    N, IA, IFAIL
C     real       A(IA,N), P(N), DP
```

## 3. Description

This routine calculates the triangular factors LU of a row permutation of a real matrix A by Gaussian elmination with partial pivoting. The rows are implicitly scaled to have largest element unity. The operations are grouped by columns for efficient working on a paged virtual machine (see [1]). *Additional precision* accumulation of inner products is not used.

## 4. References

[1] DU CROZ, J.J., NUGENT, S.M., REID, J.K. and TAYLOR, D.B.
Solving large full sets of linear equations in a paged virtual store.
ACM Trans. Math. Software., Vol. 7, pp. 527-536, 1981.

[2] STEWART, G.W.
Introduction to Matrix Computations.
Academic Press, 1973.

## 5. Parameters

N – INTEGER.

On entry, N must specify the order of the matrix.

$N > 0$.

Unchanged on exit.

A – *real* array of DIMENSION (IA,r), where $r \geq N$.

Before entry, A(I,J) must contain the matrix element $a_{IJ}$ for I,J $= 1,2,...,N$.

On successful exit, the strict upper triangle of A contains the corresponding elements of U; the lower triangle contains the multipliers used in the Gaussian elimination (it does **not** contain the matrix L as such – the subdiagonal elements are permuted). The unit diagonal elements of U are not stored.

IA – INTEGER.

On entry, IA must specify the first dimension of array A as declared in the (sub)program from which F01BTF is called.

IA $\geq$ N.

Unchanged on exit.

P – *real* array of DIMENSION at least (N).

On successful exit, P(I) contains the row index of the I(th) pivot, for I = 1,2,...,N.

DP – *real*.

On successful exit, DP contains the determinant of the permutation used, which must be either $+1.0$ or $-1.0$.

IFAIL – INTEGER.

Before entry, IFAIL must be set to 0 or 1. For users not familiar with this parameter (described in the Introduction to this Handbook) the recommended value is 0.

Unless the routine detects an error (see next section), IFAIL contains 0 on exit.

## 6. Error Indicators and Warnings

Errors detected by the routine:

IFAIL = 1

The matrix has a row consisting entirely of zeros.

IFAIL = 2

The matrix is singular or nearly singular: a pivot has been found to be less than $\frac{1}{2}b\varepsilon$ times the largest element in the corresponding row of A, where b is the base of the arithmetic and $\varepsilon$ is the relative precision (given by X02AAF).

IFAIL = 3

On entry,  N $<$ 1
or         IA $<$ N.

## 7. Accuracy

For a detailed error analysis, see [2], pp. 148-158.

## 8. Further Comments

The time taken is approximately proportional to $N^3$.

This routine may be used in combination with F04AYF to solve sets of linear equations. After a successful call of F01BTF the arrays A and P should be passed unchanged to F04AYF.

Also after a successful call of F01BTF, the determinant of A may be computed as the product of DP and A(I,I), I = 1,2,...,N.

# F02WAF

## 1. Purpose

F02WAF finds the singular values and the right-hand singular vectors (principal components) of a real rectangular $m \times n$ matrix A, where $m \geq n$.

## 2. Specification

```
      SUBROUTINE F02WAF (M, N, A, NRA, WANTB, B, SV, WORK, LWORK, IFAIL)
C     LOGICAL    WANTB
C     INTEGER    M, N, NRA, LWORK, IFAIL
C     real       A(NRA,N), B(M), SV(N), WORK(LWORK)
```

## 3. Description

The real $m \times n$ ($m \geq n$) matrix A may be factorised by the singular value decomposition (SVD) as

$$A = Q \begin{bmatrix} D \\ 0 \end{bmatrix} P^T,$$

where Q is an $m \times m$ orthogonal matrix, P is an $n \times n$ orthogonal matrix and D is the $n \times n$ diagonal matrix

$$D = \text{diag}(sv_1, sv_2, ..., sv_n),$$

with $sv_1 \geq sv_2 \geq ... \geq sv_n \geq 0$, these being the singular values of A. The first n columns of Q and the columns of P are the left- and right-hand singular vectors of A respectively.

If the matrix A is of rank r, then in exact arithmetic $sv_{r+1} = sv_{r+2} = ... = sv_n = 0$.

The routine returns the singular values, the matrix $P^T$ and optionally $Q^T b$ for a given m element vector b.

The routine first reduces A to upper triangular form by Householder transformations; the upper triangular form is then reduced to bidiagonal form by Givens plane rotations; and finally the QR algorithm is used to obtain the singular value decomposition of the bidiagonal form.

## 4. References

[1] WILKINSON, J.H.
Singular-Value Decomposition – Basic Aspects.
In 'Numerical Software – Needs and Availability.' Ed. JACOBS, D.A.H.
Academic Press, London, 1978.

## 5. Parameters

M – INTEGER.

On entry, M must specify the number of rows of A.

M $\geq$ N.

Unchanged on exit.

N – INTEGER.

On entry, N must specify the number of columns of A.

$1 \leq N \leq M$.

Unchanged on exit.

A – *real* array of DIMENSION (NRA,r) where r $\geq$ N.

Before entry, the leading M $\times$ N part of A must contain the matrix to be factorised.

On successful exit, the leading N $\times$ N part of A contains the right-hand singular vectors, stored by **rows**. The rest of the first N columns of A is used for workspace.

NRA – INTEGER.

On entry, NRA must specify the first dimension of A as declared in the (sub)program from which F02WAF is called.

NRA $\geq$ M.

Unchanged on exit.

WANTB – LOGICAL.

On entry, WANTB must be .TRUE. if $Q^Tb$ is required. If on entry WANTB is .FALSE., then B is not referenced.

Unchanged on exit.

B – *real* array of DIMENSION at least (M).

B is only referenced if WANTB is supplied as .TRUE.. In this case, before entry, B must contain the M element vector b and on successful exit B contains $Q^Tb$.

SV – *real* array of DIMENSION at least (N).

On successful exit, SV contains the N singular values of A arranged in descending order.

WORK – *real* array of DIMENSION (LWORK).

On exit, WORK(1) returns the total number of iterations taken by the QR algorithm. Otherwise WORK is used as workspace.

LWORK – INTEGER.

On entry, LWORK must specify the length of the array WORK as declared in the (sub)program from which F02WAF is called.

LWORK $\geq 3 \times$ N.

Unchanged on exit.

IFAIL – INTEGER.

Before entry, IFAIL must be set to 0 or 1. For users not familiar with this parameter (described in the Introduction to this Handbook) the recommended value is 0.

Unless the routine detects an error (see next section), IFAIL contains 0 on exit.

## 6. Error Indicators and Warnings

Errors detected by the routine:

IFAIL = 1

On entry, M $<$ N,
or         N $<$ 1,
or         NRA $<$ M,
or         LWORK $< 3 \times$ N.

IFAIL = 2

The QR algorithm has failed to converge to the singular values in $50 \times$ N iterations. The matrix A has nevertheless been factorised as $A = QCP^T$, where C is an upper bidiagonal matrix with SV(1),SV(2),...,SV(N) as its diagonal elements and WORK(2), WORK(3),..., WORK(N) as its super-diagonal elements. (This failure is not likely to occur.)

## 7. Accuracy

The computed factors Q, D and $P^T$ satisfy the relation

$$Q \begin{bmatrix} D \\ 0 \end{bmatrix} P^T = A + E,$$

where

$$\|E\|_2 \leq c \times eps \times \|A\|_2,$$

eps being the machine accuracy (see NAG Workstation Library routine X02AAF) and c being a modest function of M and N. Note that $\|A\|_2 = sv_1$.

## 8. Further Comments

The time taken is approximately proportional to $n^2(m + 6n)$.

Singular vectors associated with a zero or multiple singular value, are not uniquely determined, even in exact arithmetic, and very different results may be obtained if they are computed on different machines.

This routine is column-biased and so is suitable for use in paged environments.

If the matrix A has previously had its column means removed, then this routine provides a principal component analysis of the matrix A. The rows of the matrix $P^T$ are the principal components of A, and the singular values are the square roots of the sample variances of the observations with respect to the principal components.

# F04AYF

## 1. Purpose

F04AYF calculates the approximate solution of a set of real linear equations with multiple right-hand sides, $AX = B$, where A has been decomposed into triangular matrices using F01BTF.

## 2. Specification

```
      SUBROUTINE F04AYF (N, IR, A, IA, P, B, IB, IFAIL)
C     INTEGER    N, IR, IA, IB, IFAIL
C     real       A(IA,N), P(N), B(IB,IR)
```

## 3. Description

The routine solves $AX = B$ where A is real and B is the matrix of right-hand sides. The routine must be preceded by a call to F01BTF which calculates the triangular factorisation LU of a row permutation of A. The solution is found by permuting the rows of B, forward substitution through the lower triangular matrix L and backward substitution through U. The operations are arranged for efficiency in a paged virtual machine. *Additional precision* accumulation of inner products is **not** used.

## 4. References

[1] STEWART, G.W.
Introduction to Matrix Computations.
Academic Press, 1973.

## 5. Parameters

N – INTEGER.

On entry, N must specify the order of matrix A.

$N > 0$

Unchanged on exit.

IR – INTEGER.

On entry, IR must specify the number of right-hand sides.

Unchanged on exit.

A – *real* array of DIMENSION (IA,p) where p ≥ N.

Before entry, A must contain the decomposition, as given by F01BTF.

Unchanged on exit.

IA – INTEGER.

On entry, IA must specify the first dimension of array A as declared in the (sub)program from which F04AYF is called.

IA ≥ N

Unchanged on exit.

P – *real* array of DIMENSION at least (N).

Before entry, P must contain details of the row interchanges in the decomposition as given by F01BTF.

Unchanged on exit.

B – *real* array of DIMENSION (IB,q) where q ≥ IR.

Before entry, B must contain the IR right-hand sides.

On exit, B contains the IR solution vectors.

IB – INTEGER.

On entry, IB must specify the first dimension of array B as declared in the (sub)program from which F04AYF is called.

IB ≥ N

Unchanged on exit.

IFAIL – INTEGER.

Before entry, IFAIL must be set to 0 or 1. For users not familiar with this parameter (described in the Introduction to this Handbook) the recommended value is 0.

Unless the routine detects an error (see next section), IFAIL contains 0 on exit.

## 6. Error Indicators and Warnings

Errors detected by the routine:

IFAIL = 1

On entry, $N < 1$

or        $IA < N$

or        $IB < N$.

## 7. Accuracy

The accuracy of the computed solutions depends on the conditioning of the original matrix. For a detailed error analysis see [1], pp. 192-198.

## 8. Further Comments

The time taken is approximately proportional to $IR \times N^2$.

# F04JGF

## 1. Purpose

F04JGF finds the solution of a linear least-squares problem, $Ax = b$, where $A$ is a real $m \times n$ $(m \geq n)$ matrix and b is an m element vector. If the matrix of observations is not of full rank, then the minimal least-squares solution is returned.

## 2. Specification

```
        SUBROUTINE F04JGF (M, N, A, NRA, B, TOL, SVD, SIGMA, IRANK, WORK,
       1              LWORK, IFAIL)
C       LOGICAL    SVD
C       INTEGER    M, N, NRA, IRANK, LWORK, IFAIL
C       real       A(NRA,N), B(M), TOL, SIGMA, WORK(LWORK)
```

## 3. Description

The minimal least-squares solution of the problem $Ax = b$ is the vector x of minimum (Euclidean) length which minimizes the length of the residual vector $r = b - Ax$.

The real $m \times n$ $(m \geq n)$ matrix A is factorised as

$$A = Q \begin{bmatrix} U \\ 0 \end{bmatrix}$$

where Q is an $m \times m$ orthogonal matrix and U is an $n \times n$ upper triangular matrix. If U is of full rank, then the least-squares solution is given by

$$x = [U^{-1} \ 0] \, Q^T b.$$

If U is not of full rank, then the singular value decomposition of U is obtained so that U is factorised as

$$U = RDP^T,$$

where R and P are $n \times n$ orthogonal matrices and D is the $n \times n$ diagonal matrix

$$D = \text{diag}(sv_1, sv_2, ..., sv_n),$$

with $sv_1 \geq sv_2 \geq ... sv_n \geq 0$, these being the singular values of A. If the singular values $sv_{k+1}, ..., sv_n$ are negligible, but $sv_k$ is not negligible, relative to the data errors in A, then the rank of A is taken to be k and the minimal least-squares solution is given by

$$x = P\begin{bmatrix} S^{-1} & 0 \\ 0 & 0 \end{bmatrix}\begin{bmatrix} R^T & 0 \\ 0 & I \end{bmatrix}Q^T b,$$

where $S = \text{diag}(sv_1, sv_2, ..., sv_k)$.

The routine also returns the value of the standard error

$$\sigma = \sqrt{\frac{r^T r}{m-k}}, \quad \text{if } m > k,$$

$$= 0, \qquad\qquad \text{if } m = k,$$

$r^T r$ being the residual sum of squares and k the rank of A.

## 4. References

[1] LAWSON, C.L. and HANSON, R.J.
Solving Least-Squares Problems.
Prentice-Hall, New Jersey, 1974.

## 5. Parameters

M – INTEGER.

On entry, M must specify the number of rows of A.

$M \geq N$.

Unchanged on exit.

N – INTEGER.

On entry, N must specify the number of columns of A.

$1 \leq N \leq M$.

Unchanged on exit.

A – *real* array of DIMENSION (NRA,t) where $t \geq N$.

Before entry, the leading M × N part of A must contain the matrix to be factorised.

On successful exit, if SVD is returned as .FALSE., the leading M × N part of A, together with the first N elements of the vector WORK, contains details of the Householder QU factorisation of A. See the specification of F02WDF (in the main NAG Fortran Library Manual) for further details. If SVD is returned as .TRUE., then the top N × N part of A contains the right-hand singular vectors, stored by **rows**. The rest of the first N columns of A is used for workspace.

**NRA – INTEGER.**

On entry, NRA must specify the first dimension of A as declared in the (sub)program from which F04JGF is called.

NRA $\geq$ M.

Unchanged on exit.

**B – *real* array of DIMENSION at least (M).**

Before entry, B must contain the M element vector b.

On successful exit, the first N elements of B contain the minimal least-squares solution vector x. The remaining M $-$ N elements are used for workspace.

**TOL – *real*.**

On entry, TOL must specify a relative tolerance to be used to determine the rank of A. TOL should be chosen as approximately the largest relative error in the elements of A. For example, if the elements of A are correct to about 4 significant figures then TOL should be set to about $5 \times 10^{-4}$. See Section 8 for a description of how TOL is used to determine rank. If TOL is outside the range (eps,1.0), where eps is the machine accuracy (see NAG Workstation Library routine X02AAF), then the value eps is used in place of TOL. For most problems this is unreasonably small.

Unchanged on exit.

**SVD – LOGICAL.**

On successful exit, SVD is returned as .FALSE. if the least-squares solution has been obtained from the QU factorisation of A. In this case A is of full rank. SVD is returned as .TRUE. if the least-squares solution has been obtained from the singular value decomposition of A.

**SIGMA – *real*.**

On successful exit, SIGMA returns the value

$$\sqrt{r^T r/(M - IRANK)}$$

when M $>$ IRANK, and returns the value zero when M $=$ IRANK.

**IRANK – INTEGER.**

On successful exit, IRANK returns the rank of the matrix A. It should be noted that it is possible for IRANK to be returned as N and SVD to be returned as .TRUE.. This means that the matrix U only just failed the test for non-singularity.

WORK – *real* array of DIMENSION (LWORK).

On successful exit, if SVD is returned as .FALSE., then the first N elements of WORK contain information on the QU factorisation of A, (see parameter A above) and WORK(N+1) contains the condition number $\|U\|_E \|U^{-1}\|_E$ of the upper triangular matrix U.

If SVD is returned as .TRUE., then the first N elements of WORK contain the singular values of A arranged in descending order and WORK(N+1) contains the total number of iterations taken by the QR algorithm. Otherwise WORK is used as workspace.

LWORK – INTEGER.

On entry, LWORK must specify the dimension of the array WORK as declared in the (sub)program from which F04JGF is called.

LWORK $\geq 4 \times$ N.

Unchanged on exit.

IFAIL – INTEGER.

Before entry, IFAIL must be set to 0 or 1. For users not familiar with this parameter (described in the Introduction to this Handbook) the recommended value is 0.

Unless the routine detects an error (see next section), IFAIL contains 0 on exit.

## 6. Error Indicators and Warnings

Errors detected by the routine:

IFAIL = 1

| On entry, | N < 1, |
|---|---|
| or | M < N, |
| or | NRA < M, |
| or | LWORK < 4 × N. |

IFAIL = 2

The QR algorithm has failed to converge to the singular values in $50 \times$ N iterations. This failure can only happen when the singular value decomposition is employed, but even then it is not likely to occur.

## 7. Accuracy

The computed factors Q, U, R, D and $P^T$ satisfy the relations

$$Q\begin{bmatrix} U \\ 0 \end{bmatrix} = A + E, \quad Q\begin{bmatrix} R & 0 \\ 0 & I \end{bmatrix}\begin{bmatrix} D \\ 0 \end{bmatrix}P^T = A + F,$$

where

$$\|E\|_2 \leq c_1 \times eps \times \|A\|_2,$$

$$\|F\|_2 \leq c_2 \times eps \times \|A\|_2,$$

eps being the machine accuracy (see NAG Workstation Library routine X02AAF) and $c_1$ and $c_2$ being modest functions of m and n. Note that $\|A\|_2 = sv_1$.

For a fuller discussion, covering the accuracy of the solution x see [1], especially p. 50 and p. 95.

## 8. Further Comments

If the least-squares solution is obtained from the QU factorisation then the time taken is approximately proportional to $n^2(3m-n)$. If the least-squares solution is obtained from the singular value decomposition then the time taken is approximately proportional to $n^2(3m+19n)$. The approximate proportionality factor is the same in each case.

This routine is column biased and so is suitable for use in paged environments.

Following the QU factorisation of A the condition number

$$c(U) = \|U\|_E \|U^{-1}\|_E$$

is determined and if c(U) is such that

$$c(U) \times TOL > 1.0$$

then U is regarded as singular and the singular values of A are computed. If this test is not satisfied, U is regarded as non-singular and the rank of A is set to N. When the singular values are computed the rank of A, say k, is returned as the largest integer such that

$$sv_k > TOL \times sv_1,$$

unless $sv_1 = 0$ in which case k is returned as zero. That is, singular values which satisfy $sv_i \leq TOL \times sv_1$ are regarded as negligible because relative perturbations of order TOL can make such singular values zero.

# Answers to exercises

The following are the numerical answers for the various projects in this book. These results were obtained using single precision on a VAX–11/780 running the VMS operating system. Other answers may vary, depending upon the machine and the precision used.

## Project 1

| $x$ | Taylor Series | FORTRAN SIN |
|---|---|---|
| 0.1 | 0.3091070 | 0.3090170 |
| 2.1 | 0.3091060 | 0.3090168 |
| 4.1 | 0.3124308 | 0.3090174 |
| 6.1 | 0.7532806 | 0.3090172 |
| 8.1 | −27.30000 | 0.3090196 |
| 10.1 | 118860.7 | 0.3090184 |
| 14.1 | 1.0401101E+10 | 0.3090197 |
| 20.1 | −6.7760741E+18 | 0.3090197 |

## Project 2

| $x$ | Taylor Series | FORTRAN EXP |
|---|---|---|
| 1.0 | 2.718282 | 2.718282 |
| 5.0 | 148.4132 | 148.4132 |
| 10.0 | 22026.47 | 22026.46 |
| 15.0 | 3269018. | 3269017. |
| 20.0 | 4.8516525E+08 | 4.8516518E+08 |
| 25.0 | 7.2004911E+10 | 7.2004903E+10 |
| 30.0 | 1.0686473E+13 | 1.0686474E+13 |
| −1.0 | 0.3678794 | 0.3678795 |
| −5.0 | 6.7384299E−03 | 6.7379470E−03 |
| −10.0 | 5.9507729E−05 | 4.5399931E−05 |
| −15.0 | 2.2861121E−02 | 3.0590232E−07 |
| −20.0 | 2.903501 | 2.0611537E−09 |
| −30.0 | −26641.40 | 9.3576229E−14 |

# Project 3

The following are the roots of the quadratic for the data given. These numbers may not be easily reproducible by a single precision subroutine.

$$(i) \quad r_1 = 1, \quad r_2 = 1$$
$$(ii) \quad r_1 = 1, \quad r_2 = 3$$
$$(iii) \quad r_1 = 2.5 \times 10^{-6}, \quad r_2 = 10^5$$
$$(iv) \quad r_1 = 0.4992107, \quad r_2 = 0.5007918$$
$$(v) \quad r_1 = 0, \quad r_2 = 0$$

# Project 4

| $x$ | $p_4(x)$ | Absolute Error | Relative Error |
| --- | --- | --- | --- |
| 0.0 | 1.000000 | 0.0000000E+00 | 0.0000000E+00 |
| 0.1 | 1.527792 | 3.3599997E–06 | 2.1992521E–06 |
| 0.2 | 1.983188 | 4.1599997E–06 | 2.0976324E–06 |
| 0.3 | 2.374188 | 3.3600002E–06 | 1.4152208E–06 |
| 0.4 | 2.708792 | 1.7600001E–06 | 6.4973619E–07 |
| 0.5 | 2.995000 | 0.0000000E+00 | 0.0000000E+00 |
| 0.6 | 3.240812 | 1.4400002E–06 | 4.4433318E–07 |
| 0.7 | 3.454228 | 2.2399997E–06 | 6.4848058E–07 |
| 0.8 | 3.643248 | 2.2399997E–06 | 6.1483593E–07 |
| 0.9 | 3.815872 | 1.4400003E–06 | 3.7737126E–07 |
| 1.0 | 3.980100 | 0.0000000E+00 | 0.0000000E+00 |
| 1.1 | 4.175916 | 1.4400002E–06 | 3.4483458E–07 |
| 1.2 | 4.371340 | 2.2400000E–06 | 5.1242870E–07 |
| 1.3 | 4.566376 | 2.2400000E–06 | 4.9054216E–07 |
| 1.4 | 4.761028 | 1.4400003E–06 | 3.0245576E–07 |
| 1.5 | 4.955300 | 0.0000000E+00 | 0.0000000E+00 |
| 1.6 | 5.149209 | 1.4400002E–06 | 2.7965464E–07 |
| 1.7 | 5.342742 | 2.2400000E–06 | 4.1926032E–07 |
| 1.8 | 5.535902 | 2.2400000E–06 | 4.0463146E–07 |
| 1.9 | 5.728687 | 1.4400003E–06 | 2.5136654E–07 |
| 2.0 | 5.921100 | 0.0000000E+00 | 0.0000000E+00 |
| 2.1 | 6.113128 | 1.4399989E–06 | 2.3555843E–07 |
| 2.2 | 6.304788 | 2.2400000E–06 | 3.5528552E–07 |

| | | | |
|---|---|---|---|
| 2.3 | 6.496084 | 2.2400000E−06 | 3.4482312E−07 |
| 2.4 | 6.687020 | 1.4399989E−06 | 2.1534238E−07 |
| 2.5 | 6.877600 | 0.0000000E+00 | 0.0000000E+00 |
| 2.6 | 7.067825 | 1.4399989E−06 | 2.0374003E−07 |
| 2.7 | 7.257703 | 2.2400000E−06 | 3.0863760E−07 |
| 2.8 | 7.447238 | 2.2400000E−06 | 3.0078266E−07 |
| 2.9 | 7.636436 | 1.4399989E−06 | 1.8856950E−07 |
| 3.0 | 7.825300 | 0.0000000E+00 | 0.0000000E+00 |
| 3.1 | 8.013837 | 1.4399989E−06 | 1.7968907E−07 |
| 3.2 | 8.202051 | 2.2400000E−06 | 2.7310242E−07 |
| 3.3 | 8.389946 | 2.2400000E−06 | 2.6698621E−07 |
| 3.4 | 8.577528 | 1.4399989E−06 | 1.6788040E−07 |
| 3.5 | 8.764800 | 0.0000000E+00 | 0.0000000E+00 |
| 3.6 | 8.951769 | 1.4399989E−06 | 1.6086193E−07 |
| 3.7 | 9.138438 | 2.2400000E−06 | 2.4511846E−07 |
| 3.8 | 9.324814 | 2.2400000E−06 | 2.4021926E−07 |
| 3.9 | 9.510900 | 1.4399989E−06 | 1.5140512E−07 |
| 4.0 | 9.696700 | 0.0000000E+00 | 0.0000000E+00 |
| 4.1 | 9.882215 | 1.4399989E−06 | 1.4571621E−07 |
| 4.2 | 10.06746 | 2.2399993E−06 | 2.2249905E−07 |
| 4.3 | 10.25243 | 2.2399993E−06 | 2.1848474E−07 |
| 4.4 | 10.43714 | 1.4399989E−06 | 1.3796870E−07 |
| 4.5 | 10.62160 | 0.0000000E+00 | 0.0000000E+00 |
| 4.6 | 10.80581 | 1.7599983E−06 | 1.6287517E−07 |
| 4.7 | 10.98978 | 3.3599974E−06 | 3.0573838E−07 |
| 4.8 | 11.17351 | 4.1600001E−06 | 3.7230905E−07 |
| 4.9 | 11.35702 | 3.3599983E−06 | 2.9585215E−07 |
| 5.0 | 11.54030 | 0.0000000E+00 | 0.0000000E+00 |

# Project 5

| $x$ | $p_4(x)$ | Absolute Error | Relative Error |
|---|---|---|---|
| 0.00 | 20.00000 | 0.0000000E+00 | 0.0000000E+00 |
| 0.02 | 20.13297 | 1.6297259E−03 | 8.0948135E−05 |
| 0.04 | 20.24950 | 2.5822008E−03 | 1.2751925E−04 |
| 0.06 | 20.34966 | 3.0053118E−03 | 1.4768363E−04 |
| 0.08 | 20.43353 | 3.0287467E−03 | 1.4822431E−04 |
| 0.10 | 20.50121 | 2.7650003E−03 | 1.3487009E−04 |
| 0.12 | 20.55281 | 2.3103901E−03 | 1.1241238E−04 |

Project 5 — continued

| $x$ | $p_4(x)$ | Absolute Error | Relative Error |
|------|----------|----------------|----------------|
| 0.14 | 20.58846 | 1.7460649E–03 | 8.4807951E–05 |
| 0.16 | 20.60831 | 1.1390161E–03 | 5.5269753E–05 |
| 0.18 | 20.61253 | 5.4309017E–04 | 2.6347579E–05 |
| 0.20 | 20.60130 | 0.0000000E+00 | 0.0000000E+00 |
| 0.22 | 20.57483 | 4.5966622E–04 | 2.2341192E–05 |
| 0.24 | 20.53334 | 8.1543170E–04 | 3.9712577E–05 |
| 0.26 | 20.47706 | 1.0559203E–03 | 5.1566003E–05 |
| 0.28 | 20.40626 | 1.1778459E–03 | 5.7719826E–05 |
| 0.30 | 20.32121 | 1.1850003E–03 | 5.8313479E–05 |
| 0.32 | 20.22219 | 1.0872425E–03 | 5.3764819E–05 |
| 0.34 | 20.10953 | 8.9948782E–04 | 4.4729430E–05 |
| 0.36 | 19.98354 | 6.4069621E–04 | 3.2061194E–05 |
| 0.38 | 19.84458 | 3.3286199E–04 | 1.6773449E–05 |
| 0.40 | 19.69300 | 0.0000000E+00 | 0.0000000E+00 |
| 0.42 | 19.52919 | 3.3286150E–04 | 1.7044307E–05 |
| 0.44 | 19.35238 | 8.1543170E–04 | 4.2135998E–05 |
| 0.46 | 19.16491 | 1.0559206E–03 | 5.5096552E–05 |
| 0.48 | 18.96662 | 1.1778460E–03 | 6.2100997E–05 |
| 0.50 | 18.75796 | 1.1850004E–03 | 6.3173196E–05 |
| 0.52 | 18.53941 | 1.0872427E–03 | 5.8644950E–05 |
| 0.54 | 18.31145 | 8.9948787E–04 | 4.9121616E–05 |
| 0.56 | 18.07457 | 6.4069667E–04 | 3.5447403E–05 |
| 0.58 | 17.82929 | 3.3286246E–04 | 1.8669421E–05 |
| 0.60 | 17.57610 | 0.0000000E+00 | 0.0000000E+00 |
| 0.62 | 17.31479 | 4.5966587E–04 | 2.6547594E–05 |
| 0.64 | 17.04675 | 8.1543106E–04 | 4.7834994E–05 |
| 0.66 | 16.77256 | 1.0559204E–03 | 6.2955223E–05 |
| 0.68 | 16.49281 | 1.1778455E–03 | 7.1415714E–05 |
| 0.70 | 16.20805 | 1.1850001E–03 | 7.3111805E–05 |
| 0.72 | 15.91888 | 1.0872420E–03 | 6.8298898E–05 |
| 0.74 | 15.62586 | 8.9948776E–04 | 5.7564033E–05 |
| 0.76 | 15.32958 | 6.4069661E–04 | 4.1794799E–05 |
| 0.78 | 15.03060 | 3.3286243E–04 | 2.2145656E–05 |
| 0.80 | 14.72950 | 0.0000000E+00 | 0.0000000E+00 |
| 0.82 | 14.42686 | 3.3286147E–04 | 2.3072340E–05 |
| 0.84 | 14.12326 | 6.4069574E–04 | 4.5364588E–05 |
| 0.86 | 13.81926 | 8.9948764E–04 | 6.5089407E–05 |

| | | | |
|------|----------|------------------|------------------|
| 0.88 | 13.51546 | 1.0872422E-03 | 8.0444363E-05 |
| 0.90 | 13.21241 | 1.1849999E-03 | 8.9688394E-05 |
| 0.92 | 12.91070 | 1.1778458E-03 | 9.1230177E-05 |
| 0.94 | 12.61091 | 1.0559203E-03 | 8.3730672E-05 |
| 0.96 | 12.31362 | 8.1543205E-04 | 6.6221983E-05 |
| 0.98 | 12.01939 | 4.5966593E-04 | 3.8243714E-05 |
| 1.00 | 11.72880 | 0.0000000E+00 | 0.0000000E+00 |
| 1.02 | 11.44326 | 3.3286150E-04 | 2.9087996E-05 |
| 1.04 | 11.16254 | 6.4069580E-04 | 5.7396934E-05 |
| 1.06 | 10.88717 | 8.9948718E-04 | 8.2619023E-05 |
| 1.08 | 10.61763 | 1.0872427E-03 | 1.0239971E-04 |
| 1.10 | 10.35444 | 1.1850005E-03 | 1.1444367E-04 |
| 1.12 | 10.09808 | 1.1778462E-03 | 1.1664061E-04 |
| 1.14 | 9.849021 | 1.0559211E-03 | 1.0721076E-04 |
| 1.16 | 9.607735 | 8.1543298E-04 | 8.4872554E-05 |
| 1.18 | 9.374678 | 4.5966837E-04 | 4.9032980E-05 |
| 1.20 | 9.150300 | 0.0000000E+00 | 0.0000000E+00 |
| 1.22 | 8.935727 | 3.3286141E-04 | 3.7250626E-05 |
| 1.24 | 8.730723 | 6.4069562E-04 | 7.3384028E-05 |
| 1.26 | 8.535661 | 8.9948671E-04 | 1.0537986E-04 |
| 1.28 | 8.350889 | 1.0872411E-03 | 1.3019465E-04 |
| 1.30 | 8.176744 | 1.1849992E-03 | 1.4492313E-04 |
| 1.32 | 8.013540 | 1.1778449E-03 | 1.4698185E-04 |
| 1.34 | 7.861580 | 1.0559193E-03 | 1.3431387E-04 |
| 1.36 | 7.720417 | 6.4069551E-04 | 8.2987164E-05 |
| 1.38 | 7.592107 | 3.3286132E-04 | 4.3843076E-05 |
| 1.40 | 7.475900 | 0.0000000E+00 | 0.0000000E+00 |
| 1.42 | 7.372004 | 3.3286141E-04 | 4.5152094E-05 |
| 1.44 | 7.280604 | 6.4069737E-04 | 8.8000583E-05 |
| 1.46 | 7.201863 | 8.9948822E-04 | 1.2489660E-04 |
| 1.48 | 7.135921 | 1.0872425E-03 | 1.5236190E-04 |
| 1.50 | 7.082898 | 1.1850003E-03 | 1.6730445E-04 |
| 1.52 | 7.042591 | 1.0872426E-03 | 1.5438105E-04 |
| 1.54 | 7.015707 | 8.9948840E-04 | 1.2821067E-04 |
| 1.56 | 7.001984 | 6.4069743E-04 | 9.1502276E-05 |
| 1.58 | 7.001448 | 3.3286138E-04 | 4.7541795E-05 |
| 1.60 | 7.014100 | 0.0000000E+00 | 0.0000000E+00 |
| 1.62 | 7.039918 | 3.3286138E-04 | 4.7281996E-05 |
| 1.64 | 7.078856 | 6.4069557E-04 | 9.0508358E-05 |
| 1.66 | 7.130843 | 8.9948659E-04 | 1.2614028E-04 |

Project 5 — continued

| $x$ | $p_4(x)$ | Absolute Error | Relative Error |
|------|-----------|-----------------|-----------------|
| 1.68 | 7.195787 | 1.0872410E–03 | 1.5109411E–04 |
| 1.70 | 7.273570 | 1.1849992E–03 | 1.6291851E–04 |
| 1.72 | 7.364050 | 1.1778447E–03 | 1.5994522E–04 |
| 1.74 | 7.467064 | 1.0559192E–03 | 1.4141023E–04 |
| 1.76 | 7.582422 | 8.1543071E–04 | 1.0754225E–04 |
| 1.78 | 7.709913 | 4.5966567E–04 | 5.9620088E–05 |
| 1.80 | 7.849300 | 0.0000000E+00 | 0.0000000E+00 |
| 1.82 | 8.000324 | 5.4309296E–04 | 6.7883870E–05 |
| 1.84 | 8.162702 | 1.1390179E–03 | 1.3953932E–04 |
| 1.86 | 8.336125 | 1.7460659E–03 | 2.0945774E–04 |
| 1.88 | 8.520264 | 2.3103908E–03 | 2.7116423E–04 |
| 1.90 | 8.714763 | 2.7650006E–03 | 3.1727779E–04 |
| 1.92 | 8.919245 | 3.0287467E–03 | 3.3957436E–04 |
| 1.94 | 9.133308 | 3.0053121E–03 | 3.2904965E–04 |
| 1.96 | 9.356525 | 2.5821996E–03 | 2.7597847E–04 |
| 1.98 | 9.588447 | 1.6297247E–03 | 1.6996755E–04 |
| 2.00 | 9.828600 | 0.0000000E+00 | 0.0000000E+00 |

# Project 6

The operating range of the tricorder is $-3.6°F$ to $113.75°F$.

# Project 7

In order for MUSCLE to be competitive with SHARK, they must offer a 14.13776 per cent interest rate.

# Project 8

| Joint | Force |
|--------|---------|
| 1 | 4.222816 |
| 2 | 2.820354 |
| 3 | −1.524612 |
| 4 | 2.233369 |
| 5 | −7.220508 |

| | |
|---|---|
| 6 | −4.451278 |
| 7 | 0.722484 |
| 8 | −1.300530 |
| 9 | −5.980113 |
| 10 | −1.822598 |
| 11 | −1.822598 |
| 12 | −5.759326 |
| 13 | 0.170643 |
| 14 | 18.331112 |
| 15 | 6.258129 |
| 16 | 5.646580 |
| 17 | 16.756727 |
| 18 | −17.757778 |
| 19 | 4.967800 |
| 20 | 8.472502 |
| 21 | −10.940200 |
| 22 | −10.674385 |
| 23 | 7.624181 |
| 24 | −13.282696 |
| 25 | 19.648317 |
| 26 | −16.486187 |
| 27 | −15.159585 |

## Project 9

At 12°20′ N. 64°40′ W., the interpolated FROG value is 0.4557936, while the TOAD value there is 0.4602123.

## Project 10

| Loop | Without Auxiliary | With Auxiliary |
|---|---|---|
| 1 | 0.8164817 | 0.8317475 |
| 2 | 0.3399470 | 0.3865100 |
| 3 | 0.5508658 | 0.5889628 |
| 4 | 0.4961686 | 0.5486307 |
| 5 | 0.5315426 | 0.5697746 |
| 6 | 0.3543617 | 0.3798497 |
| 7 | 0.2990018 | 0.3773122 |
| 8 | 0.3514001 | 0.4468226 |

Project 10 — continued

| Loop | Without Auxiliary | With Auxiliary |
|------|-------------------|----------------|
| 9 | 0.1123147 | 0.2198958 |
| 10 | 0.1312859 | 0.3610834 |
| 11 | 8.7523915E–02 | 0.2407223 |
| 12 | 1.6792381E–02 | 0.1159525 |
| 13 | 5.0377142E–02 | 0.3478576 |
| 14 | 8.3961897E–02 | 0.5797627 |
| 15 | 6.8696097E–02 | 0.7470785 |
| 16 | 6.1063193E–02 | 0.8307365 |

# Project 11

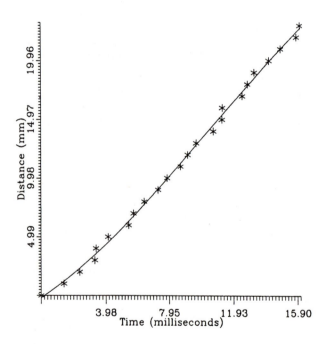

This graph describes the MOUSETRAP Motor startup response. The asterisks are the locations of the actual measurements. The curve is the quartic polynomial closest to those points in the least squares sense.

## Project 12

Answers will vary depending upon the various tolerances selected. There is no one correct answer to this problem.

## Project 13

14.93 kg of melange can be produced in one hour.

## Project 14

Prescribe 2.112264 mg of *cramerrulic* per day.

## Project 15

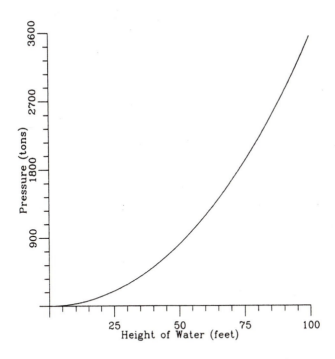

This graph describes the hydrostatic pressure of the Interpolant River Dam as a function of the height of the water behind it.

# Project 16

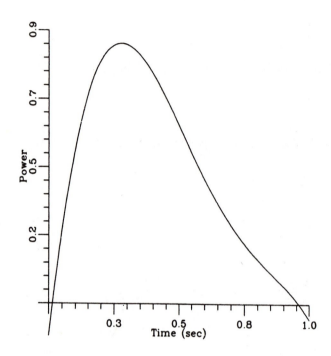

This is a graph of the power function of the laser pulse in CON ED's fusion reactor.

# Project 17

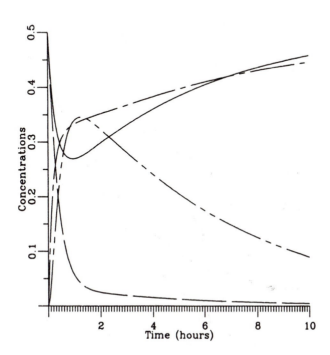

This graph shows the concentration of all four chemicals in DIRTY's plant as a function of time. The solid curve represents the concentration of *arithmetic acid*. The curve with the single gaps represents the concentration of *boundary valuum*, while the curves with the double gaps and triple gaps represent, respectively, the concentrations of the chemicals *convexitygen* and *determinantanol*.

## Project 18

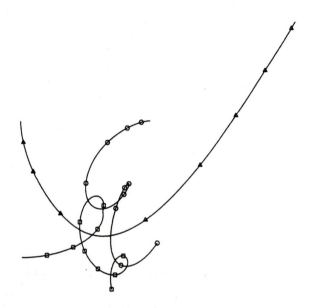

The above picture is a plot of the trajectories of the three asteroids. The curve with square markings is the trajectory of *Approximant*, while the curve with the triangular markings is the trajectory of *Barycentric*. The curve with the circular markings is the trajectory of *Chebyshev*. The markings themselves represent equal time marks. Thus, each pair of marks is one hour apart.

## Project 19

Without spraying, there will be 250.7447 million undesirable insects after seven days. Spraying any insecticide at all will cause this number to become larger.

# Project 20

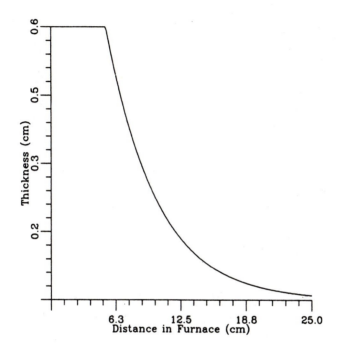

This is a plot of the radius of the silicon rod as it travels through the furnace. The speed with which the rods are pushed through the furnace should be 0.47927 cm/sec.

# Project 21

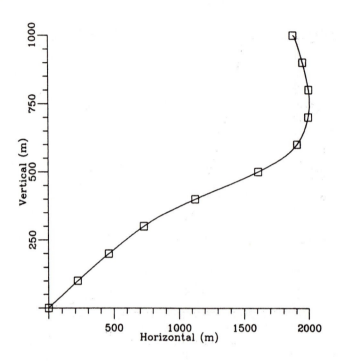

This is a graph of the trajectory of Blackford Oakes. He should jump out of
the plane when it is 1877.25 meters beyond the boat. It will then take him
247.91 seconds to reach the boat. His horizontal velocity when he lands is
8.7911 meters/second, while his vertical velocity is 4.0414 meters/second.
The square markings on the trajectory indicate equal time units.

# Project 22

The minimum cost dowel is $3027.79.

# NAG Graphical Library examples

The programs which follow can be used to produce similar graphical results to those which appear in the Answers to exercises. The comments in each of the programs explain what is going on. The programs have been written using DOUBLE PRECISION, but they may be modified to use single precision when appropriate.

## Project 11

```
      DOUBLE PRECISION C(5), R(25), Y(25), FUNCT
      EXTERNAL FUNCT
      COMMON C
C
C----- READ IN ORIGINAL POINT DATA AND CALCULATED
C      QUARTIC COEFFICIENTS
C
      OPEN (UNIT=11, FILE='PROJ11.DAT', STATUS='OLD')
      OPEN (UNIT=12, FILE='PROJ11.OUT', STATUS='OLD')
      READ (11,*) (R(IX), IX=1,24)
      READ (12,*) (C(IX), IX=1,5)
      DO 10 IX = 1, 24
         Y(IX) = IX - 1
10       CONTINUE
C
C----- INITIALIZE PLOT AND SET DATA REGION
C
      CALL J06WAF
      CALL J06WBF (0.D0, 18.D0, 0.D0, 24.D0, 1)
C
C----- DRAW AND LABEL AXES
C
      CALL J06AAF
      CALL J06AJF (1, 'TIME - MILLISECONDS')
      CALL J06AJF (2, 'DISTANCE - MILLIMETERS')
C
```

```
C----- PLOT DATA POINTS
C
      IFAIL = 0
      CALL J06BAF (R, Y, 24, 0, 2, IFAIL)
C
C----- PLOT USER FUNCTION OVER DESIRED INTERVAL
C
      CALL J06EAF (FUNCT, 0.D0, 18.D0)
C
C----- TERMINATE PLOTTING
C
      CALL J06WZF
      END
C
      DOUBLE PRECISION FUNCTION FUNCT (X)
C
C----- USER FUNCTION EVALUATES QUARTIC POLYNOMIAL
C
      DOUBLE PRECISION X, C(5), EVAL
      COMMON C
C
      EVAL = C(5)
      DO 10 I = 4, 1, -1
        EVAL = EVAL * X + C(I)
10      CONTINUE
      FUNCT = EVAL
      RETURN
      END
```

## Project 15

```
      DOUBLE PRECISION X(1000), Y(1000)
      INTEGER I, N
C
C----- READ IN DATA CALCULATED IN MAIN PROGRAM
C
      OPEN (UNIT=12, FILE='PROJ15.OUT', STATUS='OLD')
      READ (12,*) N
      READ (12,*) (X(I),Y(I),I=1,N)
C
```

```
C----- INITIALIZE PLOT AND SET DATA REGION
C
      CALL J06WAF
      CALL J06WBF (0.D0, 100.D0, 0.D0, 3600.D0, 1)
C
C----- DRAW AND LABEL AXES
C
      CALL J06AAF
      CALL J06AJF (1, 'HEIGHT OF WATER - FEET')
      CALL J06AJF (2, 'PRESSURE - TONS')
C
C----- CONNECT DATA WITH STRAIGHT LINE SEGMENTS TO DRAW PLOT
C
      IFAIL = 0
      CALL J06BAF (X, Y, N, 1, 1, IFAIL)
C
C----- TERMINATE PLOTTING
C
      CALL J06WZF
      END
```

## Project 16

```
      DOUBLE PRECISION X(1000), Y(1000)
      INTEGER I, N
C
C----- READ IN DATA CALCULATED IN MAIN PROGRAM
C
      OPEN (UNIT=12, FILE='PROJ16.OUT', STATUS='OLD')
      READ (12,*) N
      READ (12,*) (X(I), Y(I), I=1,N)
C
C----- INITIALIZE PLOT AND SET DATA REGION
C
      CALL J06WAF
      CALL J06WBF (0.D0, 1.D0, 0.D0, 1.D0, 1)
C
C----- DRAW AND LABEL AXES
C
      CALL J06AAF
```

```
      CALL J06AJF (1, 'TIME - SECONDS')
      CALL J06AJF (2, 'POWER')
C
C----- CONNECT DATA WITH STRAIGHT LINE SEGMENTS TO DRAW PLOT
C
      IFAIL = 0
      CALL J06BAF (X, Y, N, 1, 1, IFAIL)
C
C----- TERMINATE PLOTTING
C
      CALL J06WZF
      END
```

## Project 17

```
      DOUBLE PRECISION X(161), A(161), B(161), C(161),
     *              D(161)
      INTEGER I, IFAIL
      CHARACTER*15 CH(4)
      DATA CH /'ARITHMETIC ACID','BOUNDARY VALUUM',
     *          'CONVEXITYGEN   ','DETERMINANTANOL'/
C
C----- READ IN DATA CALCULATED IN MAIN PROGRAM
C
      OPEN (UNIT=12, FILE='PROJ17.OUT', STATUS='OLD')
      READ (12,*) (X(I), A(I), B(I), C(I), D(I), I=1,161)
C
C----- INITIALIZE PLOT AND SET DATA REGION
C
      CALL J06WAF
      CALL J06WBF (0.D0, 1.D1, 0.D0, .5D0, 1)
C
C----- DRAW AND LABEL AXES
C
      CALL J06AAF
      CALL J06AJF (1, 'TIME - HOURS')
      CALL J06AJF (2, 'CONCENTRATIONS')
C
C----- PLOT DATA
C
```

```
      CALL J06YMF (1)
      IFAIL = 0
      CALL J06BAF (X, A, 161, 1, 1, IFAIL)
      CALL J06YMF (2)
      IFAIL = 0
      CALL J06BAF (X, B, 161, 1, 1, IFAIL)
      CALL J06YMF (3)
      IFAIL = 0
      CALL J06BAF (X, C, 161, 1, 1, IFAIL)
      CALL J06YMF (4)
      IFAIL = 0
      CALL J06BAF (X, D, 161, 1, 1, IFAIL)
C
C----- SET UP AND PLOT KEY
C
      CALL J06WBF (0.D0, 1.D0, 0.D0, 1.D0, 0)
      CALL J06WCF (.7D0, 1.D0, .4D0, .7D0)
      IFAIL = 10
      CALL J06BYF (CH, 4, 0, IFAIL)
C
C----- TERMINATE PLOTTING
C
      CALL J06WZF
      END
```

## Project 18

```
      DOUBLE PRECISION T, X1(1200), X2(1200), X3(1200),
     *                 Y1(1200), Y2(1200), Y3(1200),
     *                 U1(12), U2(12), U3(12), V1(12),
     *                 V2(12), V3(12)
      INTEGER LINE(3), LCOL(3), MARK(3), MCOL(3), IFAIL,
     *        I, J
      CHARACTER*11 CH(3)
      DATA CH /'APPROXIMANT', 'BARYCENTRIC', 'CHEBYSHEV  '/
      DATA MARK /1, 2, 3/, MCOL /1, 1, 1/
C
C----- READ IN CALCULATED DATA
C
      OPEN (UNIT=11, FILE='PROJ18.OUT1', STATUS='OLD')
```

```
      OPEN (UNIT=12, FILE='PROJ18.OUT2', STATUS='OLD')
      I = 0
      J = 0
10    CONTINUE
      I = I + 1
      READ (11,*,END=20) T, X1(I), Y1(I), X2(I), Y2(I),
     *                   X3(I), Y3(I)
      GOTO 10
20    CONTINUE
      J = J + 1
      READ (12,*,END=30) T, U1(J), V1(J), U2(J), V2(J),
     *                   U3(J), V3(J)
      GOTO 20
30    CONTINUE
C
C----- INITIALIZE PLOT AND SET DATA REGION
C
      CALL J06WAF
      CALL J06WBF (0.D0, 2.1D6, -1.D5, 2.D6, 1)
C
C----- DRAW AND LABEL AXES
C
      CALL J06AAF
C
C----- PLOT HOURLY MARKERS
C
      IFAIL = 0
      CALL J06BAF (U1, V1, J-1, 0, 1, IFAIL)
      IFAIL = 0
      CALL J06BAF (U2, V2, J-1, 0, 2, IFAIL)
      IFAIL = 0
      CALL J06BAF (U3, V3, J-1, 0, 3, IFAIL)
C
C----- PLOT ASTEROID PATHS
C
      IFAIL = 0
      CALL J06BAF (X1, Y1, I-1, 1, 1, IFAIL)
      IFAIL = 0
      CALL J06BAF (X2, Y2, I-1, 1, 2, IFAIL)
      IFAIL = 0
```

```
      CALL J06BAF (X3, Y3, I-1, 1, 3, IFAIL)
C
C----- SET UP KEY FOR MARKERS
C
      CALL J06WBF (0.D0, 1.D0, 0.D0, 1.D0, 0)
      CALL J06WCF (.2D0, .45D0, .6D0, .9D0)
      IFAIL = 0
      CALL J06BZF (CH, 2, 3, 0, LINE, LCOL, MARK,
     *             MCOL, IFAIL)
C
C----- TERMINATE PLOTTING
C
      CALL J06WZF
      END
```

## Project 20

```
      DOUBLE PRECISION X(1000), Y(1000)
      INTEGER I, N
C
C----- READ IN DATA CALCULATED IN MAIN PROGRAM
C
      OPEN (UNIT=12, FILE='PROJ20.OUT', STATUS='OLD')
      READ (12,*) N
      READ (12,*) (X(I), Y(I), I=1,N)
C
C----- INITIALIZE PLOT AND SET DATA REGION
C
      CALL J06WAF
      CALL J06WBF (0.D0, 25.D0, 0.D0, .6D0, 1)
C
C----- DRAW AND LABEL AXES
C
      CALL J06AAF
      CALL J06AJF (1, 'DISTANCE IN FURNACE - CM')
      CALL J06AJF (2, 'THICKNESS - CM')
C
C----- CONNECT DATA WITH STRAIGHT LINE SEGMENTS TO DRAW PLOT
C
      IFAIL = 0
```

```
      CALL J06BAF (X, Y, N, 1, 1, IFAIL)
C
C----- TERMINATE PLOTTING
C
      CALL J06WZF
      END
```

## Project 21

```
      DOUBLE PRECISION X(1000), Y(1000), U(11), V(11)
      INTEGER I, N, J, INCR
C
C----- READ IN DATA CALCULATED IN MAIN PROGRAM
C
      OPEN (UNIT=12, FILE='PROJ21.OUT', STATUS='OLD')
      READ (12,*) N
      READ (12,*) (X(I),Y(I), I=1,N)
C
C----- SET UP ARRAYS WHERE MARKERS WILL BE PLACED
C
      I = 1
      INCR = (N-1) / 10
      DO 10 J = 1, 11
        U(J) = X(I)
        V(J) = Y(I)
        I = I + INCR
10      CONTINUE
C
C----- INITIALIZE PLOT AND SET DATA REGION
C
      CALL J06WAF
      CALL J06WBF (0.D0, 2.D3, 0.D0, 1.D3, 1)
C
C----- DRAW AND LABEL AXES
C
      CALL J06AAF
      CALL J06AJF (1, 'HORIZONTAL - METERS')
      CALL J06AJF (2, 'VERTICAL - METERS')
C
C----- CONNECT DATA WITH STRAIGHT LINE SEGMENTS TO
```

```
C         DRAW PLOT, DRAW EQUAL TIME MARKERS
C
          IFAIL = 0
          CALL J06BAF (X, Y, N, 1, 1, IFAIL)
          CALL J06BAF (U, V, 11, 0, 3, IFAIL)
C
C----- TERMINATE PLOTTING
C
          CALL J06WZF
          END
```

# Index